# DEVELOPING FEEDBACK FOR PUPIL LEARNING

Feedback is often considered to be one of the pivotal enablers of formative assessment. This key topic has received considerable attention within research literature and has been studied by a number of leading experts in the field. This book is positioned at the heart of these debates and offers a specific contribution to 'exploring' and 'exploiting' the learning gap which feedback seeks to shift.

*Developing Feedback for Pupil Learning* seeks to synthesise what we know about feedback and learning into more in-depth understandings of what influences both the structure of and changes to the learning gap. This research-informed but accessibly written enquiry is at the very heart of teaching, learning and assessment. It offers a timely contribution to understanding what works (and what doesn't) for whom and why. Split into three main parts, it covers:

- feedback for learning in theory, policy and practice;
- conceptualising the 'learning gap';
- new futures for feedback.

This text will be essential reading for students, teachers, researchers and all those who engage with issues related to teaching, learning and assessment academically.

**Ruth Dann** is Senior Lecturer in Education at University College London, Institute of Education, UK.

# DEVELOPING FEEDBACK FOR PUPIL LEARNING

Teaching, Learning and Assessment in Schools

*Ruth Dann*

Routledge
Taylor & Francis Group

LONDON AND NEW YORK

First published 2018
by Routledge
2 Park Square, Milton Park, Abingdon, Oxon OX14 4RN

and by Routledge
711 Third Avenue, New York, NY 10017

*Routledge is an imprint of the Taylor & Francis Group, an informa business*

*British Library Cataloguing in Publication Data*
A catalogue record for this book is available from the British Library

*Library of Congress Cataloging in Publication Data*
A catalog record for this book has been requested

ISBN: 978-1-138-68101-9 (hbk)
ISBN: 978-1-138-68102-6 (pbk)
ISBN: 978-1-315-56421-0 (ebk)

Typeset in Bembo
by Taylor & Francis Books

Printed and bound by CPI Group (UK) Ltd, Croydon, CR0 4YY

**For Mark**

# CONTENTS

**PART III**
## New futures for feedback                                     **113**

# INTRODUCTION

Feedback is often considered to be one of the pivotal enablers of formative assessment. It has received considerable attention in the research literature. Hattie's (2009) seminal work of meta-analysis contributes to our understanding of the enormous potential that feedback has for enhancing pupil learning. Black and Wiliam's (1998a) and Shute's (2008) work illustrate just two of the large review studies seeking to critique and explore feedback practices, exposing their effectiveness. Yet the fundamental basis of feedback, established by Ramaprasad (1983) and Sadler (1989), is that feedback is designed to alter a 'learning gap'. However, a fundamental understanding of what 'the learning gap' is, how it might be constructed, how it is altered and regulated, and by whom, is missing from the literature in any substantial and sustained way. Torrance (2012) calls for the need to 'explore and exploit' the learning gap, rather than seek to close it in simple linear ways. Closer inspection of some of the research literature on feedback also exposes that different types of feedback may not always yield such positive effects on those for whom it is intended (Kluger and DeNisi, 1996). This book is positioned within these debates, and offers a specific contribution to 'exploring' and 'exploiting' the learning gap that feedback seeks to shift.

The book is grounded in contemporary international policy contexts in which performance in the internationally competitive global market increasingly shapes education at a national level. As Hursh (2013), Lingard (2010) and Ozga (2009) argue, national policies become increasingly shaped and steered by global educational policy agendas. Even classroom processes become increasingly distorted to serve these larger policy directions. Thus, in a policy climate in which evidence of pupil learning, and the best way to achieve such learning, become the essence of school accountability, any process that seems to offer gains in learning is likely to be hijacked by game-playing tactics. Feedback seems to have succumbed to such tactics and is increasingly precisely constructed and focused on nationally tested learning outcomes and levels (Dann, 2015, Murtagh, 2014; Torrance, 2012). Despite its potential to be 'effective', it is clearly not effective for all pupils. Whether in the USA or UK, standards of learning do not rise in the same way for all pupils. There are certainly many possible factors for this. If feedback is to be considered to be an 'effective' and positive strategy, it needs to be understood in more nuanced ways.

If feedback is about changing the learning gap to help pupils move from what they learn now to learning something different, there must be a notion of a learning gap. However, who constructs this gap, and who controls it may be more complex than much of the research currently reveals. The first three chapters of this book seek to examine the national and international policy context in which teaching, assessment and learning operate. It examines how teaching and learning interrelate within assessment, as well as the current research evidence on feedback. This first part of the book serves an essential context-shaping purpose, drawing from theory and policy which frames the remainder of the book.

The second section of the book seeks to examine the national and international policy context in which teaching, assessment and learning operate. How this gap is understood and controlled by different participants, in different contexts and in different ways forms the focus of chapters 4, 5 and 6. Three distinctive conceptualisations of the learning gap are offered which look differently at influences on and approaches to framing the learning gap. These are the 'deterministic approach' (chapter 4) in which the learning gap is largely determined by national or international agendas. The learning gap in this chapter applies as much to a system level, where the gap is between individual school performances in national league tables, and between the performances of different countries identified through international comparative measures such as PISA (Programme for International Student Assessment), as it does to a learning level for pupils.

Chapter 5 constructs a 'relational approach' to understanding the learning gap. This chapter draws from constructivist theory, and uses Vygotsky's notion of the Zone of Proximal Development (ZPD) as the starting point for framing a space in which learning develops from 'now' to 'next'. It considers how teaching and learning become a relational communicative encounter in which multidirectional feedback practices play a significant part.

Chapter 6 presents an 'individualistic approach', where each pupil's own understanding of his/her future learning, as well as processes of internalising learning, are examined as essential components of the learning gap. An individual's interpretation of feedback within this approach cannot be separated from self-regulatory processes which pupils use to regulate their own learning trajectories. Chapter 7 provides a case study in which pupils (aged 9–10) who have struggled to meet expected standards of learning make sense of feedback. It explores the ways in which teachers use and interpret feedback in classroom contexts. It also exposes the different ways in which the learning gap is constructed and regulated by different participants. This raises particular implications which form the focus of the final section of the book.

The final part of this book focuses on new possibilities for using and understanding feedback (chapters 8 and 9). It challenges simple notions of linearly shaping the learning gap in ways which can easily be managed and systemised across the school system. It brings pupils' understanding and participation centre stage, and seeks to clarify how teaching and learning can be better aligned through use of feedback dialogues. It offers some essential principles for understanding feedback and offers suggestions for innovative new practices.

The book is constructed to build an argument across its chapters. However, each chapter is sufficiently shaped that it can be read discretely. The intention of this book is to offer rigorous, in-depth and serious consideration of the notion of feedback. It does so by giving due regard to theory, policy and practice, which, current research suggests, all bear heavily on the ways in which feedback is constructed, enacted and interpreted. It is hoped that the arguments offered in this book will open the way for further research, which can be used to develop feedback as a way of further enhancing approaches to formative assessment. The significant contribution of this book relates to the way in which pupils are located and given agency in the feedback process. Their understanding and engagement needs to be explored rather than assumed. Furthermore, what they bring to the process of feedback cannot be ignored, but should be part of the discussions about *their* future learning.

# PART I

# Feedback for learning in theory, policy and practice

# 1

# FRAMING LEARNING IN NATIONAL AND INTERNATIONAL ASSESSMENT POLICY CONTEXTS

## Chapter overview

Assessment is centre stage within global education systems. Ostensibly the power of high-stakes global comparative testing systems, such as the Programme for International Student Assessment (PISA), Trends in International Mathematics and Science (TiMMs), and Progress in International Reading and Literacy (PIRLS), are used as signifiers of a nation's educational performance, which lead to assessment shaping global educational systems (Au, 2011; Lingard, 2010; Tanner, 2013). Furthermore, in England, a national testing framework, as well as formal examinations at age 16, are used as powerful indicators of school and teacher success. Overall, the dominant paradigm of assessment is summative, serving the purposes of accountability. Successes in learning from our education systems are therefore seen largely through the lens of standardised testing.

It is important to understand the significance of this form of assessment, and its use in national and global interpretations of how specific learning outcomes are characterised and measured. It is only through understanding how and why this form of assessment prevails that the argument that is developed as the central strand of this book can be usefully positioned. This chapter thus provides an important foregrounding for some of the classroom-focused practices that are explored. Additionally, it adds a rationale for a different approach to understanding and supporting pupils' learning, through feedback, which is subsequently examined.

## Educational purpose

There seems little question that education is important. Schooling is compulsory across the developed world and in part of the Sustainable Development Goals across the globe. In England, even in times of economic recession, and significant government cutbacks, the education budget has been protected. Policy narratives stress the importance of education for the development of the economy. Driving up educational standards is part of national policy on securing continual and growing presence in the competitive global market (DfE, 2010 and 2016).

England is not alone in locating education as a central player in economic success. The United States of America and Australia, for example, have similar policy aspirations. If education is given such centre stage, it is clear that the high levels of funding given to it must be accounted for and seen to be effective. The need to demonstrate the success of education policy and expenditure becomes an important strand of developing and sustaining an education system. Education, therefore, has to become both visible and measurable in order to show the impact of education policy and expenditure. Allied to these requirements, the formation of a national curriculum with accompanying testing, offers structure and evidence to frame such a policy.

More fundamental to this argument is the essence of the education that is offered. Since national agendas are increasingly pulled in the direction of international priorities, there is a particular leaning towards the curriculum areas that are highlighted in international educational comparative statistics. Hence a national curriculum that is designed to be broad and balanced becomes weighted in particular ways. Policy arguments alone do not account for such weighting. There are more educationally grounded perspectives. Perhaps of most significance in the USA and England is E. D. Hirsch's argument for core knowledge being particularly prominent in the national curriculum (Gibbs, 2015; Hirsch, 2006). Specific weightings given in the curriculum are of significance as part of the values and priorities placed on the content of learning within compulsory schooling. Such values and priorities are part of the cultural values and beliefs of a country, selected for the next generation to learn.

Although this national policy-driven account may offer a particular story for the priorities of the education system, it is far from complete and very far from meeting with universal approval. Underpinning such policy priorities are a range of assumptions and conceptions that are challenged and critiqued across the educational sector. It is not the priority of this book to give sufficient account of such challenges. Albeit here, the purpose of a brief critique is to place this policy setting in an arena in which other thinking and other ways of being and doing can be constructed and enacted. These offer different understandings of learning and what it means to be a learner.

## The commodification of learning

Central to the notion of schooling is the idea that something will be learnt. The importance of learning is thus central. But what learning is, and who or what it is for, is not straightforward. As education became compulsory in the late nineteenth century, concerns were focused on the importance of education, notably the 3Rs, for an increasingly industrialised society and economy. The importance of raising the standards of education through inspection processes loomed large even in these early days. The system of Payment by Result in 1862, designed to reward effective teaching, was met with attempts to 'game' the system. This resulted in a narrowing of the curriculum. Even the inspection system had to work differently in bowing down to the supremacy of the examination data, as Matthew Arnold, chief inspector reported:

> The new examination groups the children by its standards, not by their classes; and however much we may strive to make the standards correspond with the classes, we cannot make them correspond at all exactly … He hears every child in the group before him read, and so far his examination is more complete than the old inspection. But he does not question them; he does not, as an examiner under the rule of the six standards, go beyond the three matters, reading, writing, and arithmetic, and the amount of these three matters which the standards themselves prescribe; and, indeed, the entries for grammar, geography, and history, have now altogether disappeared from the forms of report furnished to the inspector. The nearer, therefore, he gets to the top of the school the more does his examination, in itself, become an inadequate means of testing the real attainments and intellectual life of the scholars before him.
>
> (Arnold, 1908: 93)

The nature of learning, even in the early days of schooling, became intricately caught up in attempts to make it accountable. However, alongside the increasing pressure to make schools accountable were other agendas. Lowndes (1937) wrote of the 'Silent Social Revolution' in which he argued that early schooling was as much about social discipline and the calming of society in the midst of urban growth as about notions of specific knowledge to be learnt. Indeed, 'Education has become a principal foundation of practically every new activity in the community' (245). The purpose of education was thus promoted as a form of social control as well as cultural expansion. These early examples of shaping learning for particular purposes, serve to illustrate that understanding learning in the context of education is not straightforward, and has been much contested. Hanson (1993: 5) takes the notion of social control even further. In relation to the use of tests, not only do they become a means for providing evidence for accountability, but they 'enlist people as willing accomplices in their own surveillance and domination'.

It was not until James Callaghan's Ruskin Speech in October 1976, that the content of the curriculum in England became a matter for national concern, and subsequently control. The focus of learning became more related to content to be acquired than to notions of who was learning and how they might experience their education. With a declining budget for education, efficiency became even more important. A decade later the National Curriculum (1988) brought the nationalisation of the curriculum and the predefining of learning outcomes for children across the compulsory school sector. Although it presented a coherent curriculum for all, the leading role of assessment in shaping the curriculum illustrated that prevailing considerations were rather more about accountability and standards (Haviland, 1988; Lawton and Chitty, 1988). Furthermore, accountability shifted away from being to the public to being to the government as its regulator (Biesta, 2004: 240). This is further explored in the next chapter.

With a legacy of an education system using tests for school selection before comprehensive schooling, and the renewed use of tests for accountability accompanying the National Curriculum, England was influential in the use of testing internationally. Indeed, White (2014) argues that many of the countries that are currently highest ranking in international educational comparative tests scores have drawn their own systems from England. Priorities given to particular subjects, measured in particular ways, have thus become dominant, with other countries better shaping their systems (fashioned on the English system) to perform well in tests. Such a legacy seems to make it currently more difficult for other ways of shaping education to have credibility.

Extending such contemporary debate, Biesta (2006) has sustained consideration of fundamental questions of what or who learning is for. With little choice over what is given priority in the curriculum, complex decisions over what we teach and why, often become marginalised from debate. As Foucault recognises (2002 /1972: 28), we soon seem to accept the knowledge that is set out for us, and do not question why it is there, and whether it could be different. The fact that it is not agreed within a school, or between teachers and learners, but based on external decisions and constructions seems to get lost. Thus, not only do teachers soon lose interest in disrupting and questioning what counts as knowledge, but pupils too receive the content without much legitimate scope for having their own views or being able to drive their own interests. The content of learning thus becomes presented as fact rather than as constructions of knowledge. There are arguments for why this may be useful, E.D. Hirsch's contribution, being a particular example. Such arguments are developed further in chapters 2 and 4.

Of further concern is that our curriculum therefore makes learning a very particular and focused endeavour mainly concerned with 'having' specific knowledge. Biesta (2006) signals the danger of an approach to learning that he terms 'learnification'. He warns that as learning has become so central within policy, it has marginalised and pushed out broader ideas of education. Its centrality has also been characterised by a particular 'language of learning'. The cause of this shift has been varied and the result of many changing priorities. Amongst these is the increasing emphasis on learning outcomes, so that teaching is seen as being about measuring and being accountable for learning outcomes. Most teachers in England have their 'performance management' linked to targets for pupil attainment outcomes. Their success and progress thus become dependent on their pupils' results. This certainly steers what counts as learning in classrooms in particular ways. The relationship of teaching, learning and assessment is further analysed in more detail in the next chapter.

Biesta (2006: 20–21) argues that learning across all sectors of education has become commodified, and part of an economic transaction. Here the learner is identified as having particular needs, and the teacher in the institution provides for these needs. Although in some senses this should be part of education, what seems to prevail is that this way of seeing the relationship between teaching and learning becomes education itself. It is thus pre-determined, rendering education to be where the learner gains the particular pre-defined learning which s/he is lacking. Little acknowledgement is given to the experiences and insights that each child brings to their educational encounter. Indeed, this may even be seen to contaminate rather than enrich the standards that are valued nationally and globally.

## Measurement of learning, and its impact in classrooms

The importance of the prized educational standards that are seen to matter most are born from the national and international data sets that are used to reflect each nation's educational success both within national policy and international comparative data. As schools are positioned against national benchmarks, and countries pitched against each other on the competitive educational arena, the curriculum slowly becomes more shaped to reflect the priorities of this national and global 'game playing'.

Standardised testing has notably been the tool through which national and global comparisons are made. Accordingly, their increasingly high-stakes role has had a significant impact on learning in schools. Koretz (2008: 251) identifies seven ways in which schools/teachers make adjustments in order to maximise test results:

- working more effectively;
- teaching more;
- working harder;
- reallocation (moving resources to better match test content);
- alignment (matching teaching more specifically to test content);
- coaching (giving specific instruction to small details of taking a test, e.g. eliminating wrong answers first from multiple-choice questions);
- cheating (e.g. providing answers or hints to students during the test, or changing answers).

Such responses by teachers are evident due to the way results are used and the implications of the scores for accountability. They reveal direct links between testing and classroom practice. Some may be considered beneficial, others clearly result only in raising test scores. As this book begins to unravel, the impact of testing priorities also begins to shape the focus and type of feedback given to children.

Standardised testing potentially offers a good way of providing data on what has been attained in a way that offers least bias and greatest validity and reliability. However, distortions leading to grade inflation (higher results that do not relate to increased learning) are particular possibilities. All too often the results from standardised testing (undertaken under particular uniform conditions) are used to reflect aspects of the education system which they are not intended to measure. As Koretz so aptly points out, standardised tests select from the 'domain' that they are intended to test. Thus they give only a representation of what has been attained. Ensuring that a domain is adequately reflected in a test is not a simple matter. The number of items must be balanced against the length of the test. The type of question, and whether its language or requirements introduce bias, might give some pupils (or groups of pupils) an unfair advantage or disadvantage. The scoring or marking of the test must also be considered so that the reliability of the markers is consistent within a test, and across different markers. 'Any standardised test is merely a planned set of compromises, and cannot be perfectly reliable and valid! A test, even a good one, is always just a test: a valuable source of information, but still only limited and a particular view of student performance' (316). For this reason, Koretz indicates that the result of a test should not be considered in isolation from other forms of evidence about attainment. Unfortunately, this is seldom heeded.

The context in which tests are framed is also important. Tests were often related to norm-referenced standards. This meant that a sample of results were captured that were thought to reflect a 'norm group'. Results were consequently compared with this 'normal sample' so that each school result was referenced to this comparative group. In England, end of key stage results for each school were set alongside national averages, which effectively acted as a comparative norm. Percentage scores of pupils reaching particular levels in relation to benchmarks became the format of reporting. However, since 'levels' were removed from the national system (DfE, 2015) reporting changed. National measurements then became linked to particular standards. These formed from clear nationally determined expectations of the knowledge that should be reached at particular stages in schooling. Reporting of results therefore linked to the extent to which particular standards had been reached or exceeded. Typically the language used in reporting standards assessment links to an 'expected' or 'proficient' standard that pupils match, fall below, or are significantly above. In England (in 2016) a scaled score based on assessment or testing results was used to determine whether or not a pupil was within the expected category or not. Of course, the way the test results are scaled, and the decisions made over what standard is expected, are nationally determined. These can be adjusted each year. It makes comparisons year on year potentially unreliable.

The importance for a pupil to reach the expected standard, and for a school to have the greatest percentage of pupils possible at or above the expected standard, becomes essential. This returns us to the impact of these tests and measurements on classroom practices. In the United States it has been very clear that defining standards will focus teaching to precisely ensure that these standards are met. The agenda of pushing teaching towards the content of what is tested is not necessarily an unintended consequence. Popham (1987) was a particular advocate of 'measurement driven instruction' (MDI), which was further promoted by Madaus (1988). The drive in the UK for standards to be increased for all children, and evidenced through the outcomes of national tests, reveals that the focus on a narrowly defined core curriculum is intentional. This is despite the broader terms and aims of the National Curriculum. The reality that schools are increasingly judged on test and examination data gives further evidence that what leads to the best data possible must be most important. The presumed causal link between teaching to the test and better test outcomes may not be quite so linear as it may seem. Classroom practices that sharply focus on particular curriculum outcomes may lead to better outcomes – however, they may not. The focus in this book on feedback reveals that feedback is often far more focused and linked to particular success criteria, and is mainly in the subjects that are tested in national tests, particularly at the primary school level. This reflects much of the research evidence base for feedback (outlined in chapter 3). However, standards are not soaring, and simple solutions to raising standards through more focused teaching practices (including feedback) do not seem to have the uniform outcomes of raising attainment across the pupil population. Understanding why this might be and how we could understand teaching and learning differently, using feedback as the communication tool between both, provides the essence of this book.

It has become far clearer that the drive for school improvement, through the use of pupil performance data as key evidence of school quality, raises the importance of pupil learning within schools. However, as already indicated, it often does so in a way that commodifies learning, and to a large degree dehumanises it. Indicators of learning, seen largely through test and formal examination data, are aggregated to give percentages. Individual pupils become less significant in such aggregated data. This leads to groups of pupils who are identified as not adequately performing becoming a problem, for the school as well as for individual teachers (Pratt, 2016).

The extent to which lower achieving pupils become a problem is particularly illustrated through Hill et al.'s (2016) study looking into types of head teachers in 411 UK Academy schools (separated from local authority control). Cook (2016) reports on this study that some head teachers, given the typology label as 'surgeons', are often brought in for a short term to turn around a failing school. They remove (expel) on average 28 per cent of the lowest achieving final year pupils taking age 16 examinations. This has the effect of raising the percentage examination result scores for the school. However, this increased school performance has little more than a two- or three-year positive effect for the school. It illustrates that pupils, under this form of leadership, are valued only for the achievement scores they can bring to the school.

Further indication that some schools closely link their school priorities to testing and examination priorities relates to a study undertaken by the Office for Standards in Education (Ofsted, 2015: 5) examining Key Stage 3 (11–14 year olds). In one in five school inspections 'the quality of teaching and the rate of pupils' progress and achievement were not good enough' in KS3. The explanation offered was the 'lack of priority given to Key Stage 3 by many secondary school leaders'. Schools reported that staffing priorities were given to Key Stages 4 and 5 in which the examined attainments of the pupils were of greater significance for the judgements made about school success. Thus, lessons in KS3 were often taken by non-specialist teachers. Furthermore, insufficient effort was made to liaise with feeder primary schools to ensure that existing learning was built upon. This report gives further illustration of the reality that, in some schools, priority is given to what (and who) counts in terms of yielding data in high-stakes events.

## Different possibilities

However, a link between raising school success and regarding learning and learners as commodities does not permeate the whole school system. There are other ways of raising standards so that schools are successful, so that the lives and learning of pupils are also enhanced and energised. National policy requiring high levels of achievement can be achieved in ways which value pupils and what they bring to their educational experience. This offers a notion of education in different ethical terms. Here the values that underpin what might be considered 'effective' and 'successful' are considered differently. Biesta (2010) draws attention to this distinction in his argument for 'good education in an age of measurement'. He highlights that education is a moral rather than a technical practice, and highlights the importance of professionals not only thinking about the effectiveness of their actions, but also the educational value of what they do (36).

Some of the ideas and research data offered in this book seek to reveal that there are different ways of seeking learning, teaching and assessment that position pupils very differently in educative processes, for different reasons. They too can yield successful learning outcomes, even in national and global standardised contexts. The spirit of this book rests on the premise that pupils matter, both their lives and their learning. Teaching and learning (as well as teachers and pupils) are part of a relational dynamic. The role of feedback is positioned as an important component (whether intentional or unintentional) in this process. Chapter 2 further explores the interrelation of teaching, learning and assessment in more detail. However, the key point for this chapter is that the demands of national and assessment policy drivers, with the needs for visible measured standards, can be incorporated into school structures and systems in more humane ways. Indeed, unless there is a way to position different perspectives into and alongside national demands they are unlikely to be considered relevant. Schools must be able to deliver national priorities, and perform successfully in the regimes of surveillance and inspection to which they are subjected.

## The importance of pupils

Of particular concern in the education systems in both England and the USA in particular, is the increasing gap between the achievements of pupils from differing social classes. The persistent failure to narrow this gap has promoted policies that seek to address this issue. The No Child Left Behind policy in the USA and the government White Paper in the UK (*Education Excellence Everywhere*, DfE, 2016) steer education policy towards seeking to ensure that all pupils achieve. The policy discourse raises the profile of all pupils, but particularly those that might previously have been more marginalised from gaining nationally expected attainments. By raising expectations for all pupils, classroom practices have needed to engage rather than exclude pupils. For many, who look to the long-term improvement of their schools, a different type of learning environment is being created. Although the ultimate aim is to ensure that the standards (as revealed through tests) rise, they are enacting such changes through approaches which bring the individual pupil centre stage.

As part of this narrative, the ways in which pupils learn, as well as the formative assessment that can help to understand and steer pathways towards future learning, gains increasing attention. Wiliam (2016) is so bold as to claim that formative assessment should be the basis for school improvement, teachers' own professional development, as well as pupils' learning. He claims 'students do not necessarily – or even generally – learn exactly what they are taught and that, to be effective, teachers have to find out what their students actually did learn before moving on' (100). He further points to the importance of the quality of the evidence teachers glean about their pupils' learning. Framing what pupils should know through a more tightly focused national curriculum, expected attainment outcome measures or in precise lessons structures, does not mean that these attainments will be reached. Locating the pupils more centrally in education, and enriching rather than constraining their learning experiences, can be seen as a particular approach to raising national attainment levels. Crucial to this approach for 'effective' education, pupil response and active engagement are required.

In this book it is essential to establish footings for building an argument in which pupil agency is promoted as part of the way that national (and international) priorities for raising standards can be achieved. Schools in England (as in the US) whose attainment results are not sufficiently high are likely to be placed in a category of failure by the inspectorate system. This often results in a new head teacher, and staff changes, whose immediate aim must be to raise standards. Already highlighted are the 'super-heads', characterised as 'surgeons' who fulfil the remit of raising standards, who seem to have little regard for the pupils who are considered to be the greatest problem to achieving the desired increase in results. However, there are altogether different types of head teachers who transform schools in very different ways, and who take up Biesta's mantra of aligning high standards with high moral purpose. They recognise that children need to be understood in the complexity of their own lives and circumstances. Peacock (2016) writes of her own transformation of a school in Wroxham that had been categorised as 'failing' for three years. Her premise as she led it to the category of 'outstanding' was to draw on Hart et al.'s (2004) notion of 'learning without limits'. Here, learning futures are identified as less predictable and are not bounded by fixed notions. Trust is developed amongst staff, and with children. Both are seen to have agency in their educational encounter. Peacock extends this concept to embrace assessment, teasing out her thinking on 'assessment for learning without limits'. Essential here is to 'engage in dialogue that informs future learning and assessment where no one is labelled or limited' (5). She suggests that her approach may be seen as swimming against the tide (98) when conformity and narrowness of teaching to the tests seem to prevail. Peacock particularly highlights the importance of ensuring that a broad and balanced curriculum is offered both in and beyond the classroom. Although this is supposedly the primary aim of the English National Curriculum (2014), its translation into classrooms seems far less evident in practice.

The importance of preserving and promoting a broad and balanced curriculum was also a primary finding from a research project carried out in an area of high deprivation in England (Shain et al., 2016). In a sample of schools which had been rated as outstanding, and two schools that had been in a category of failure, the transformation towards more successful outcomes had been closely linked to deliberate attempts to broaden (rather than limit) the learning experiences of the children. Assessment was focused on individual pupils' actual achievements which were directly linked to how they were supported in their ongoing experience in the school. There was 'recognition of the uniqueness of the pupil within the formal curriculum, through the detailed, focused and regular assessment of progress and attainment, as well as through the enriched opportunities provided in and after school' (Dann, 2016b: 29). The priority of linking a breadth to learning with the detail of formative assessment was clearly evident as a complex process, which would alter within and between classes.

This book seeks to explore the interactions between teachers and pupils through the use of feedback for learning. The premise is that the educational encounter is not one of simple solutions. It is not based on rules but on relationships. Formative assessment is based in classrooms, where pupils and teachers interact. It is part of how we might better see our likely progress in terms of developing pupils' future learning. This is clearly linked to national and global standards, but not controlled by them. This book offers no short-term fixes. Its concern is with developing a more relational approach to understanding feedback as a process which is designed to better align teachers and learners in the pursuit of learning for them both. The nature of the relationship of teaching, learning and assessment requires more in-depth understanding as part of the context in which feedback for learning is established, developed and sustained. This is the focus of the following chapter.

# 2

# THE RELATIONSHIP BETWEEN TEACHING, LEARNING AND ASSESSMENT

## Chapter overview

This chapter is important in foregrounding issues related to national and international policy contexts in which teaching, learning and assessment co-exist. It builds on the previous chapter by seeking to explore ways in which teaching, assessment and learning interrelate, as different assessment and curriculum priorities and practices are required or sought. Particular emphasis is given to the ways in which national and international testing requirements influence teaching and learning relationships. Part of the discussion examines particular discourses related to who teaching is for, what learning success looks like, and what (or who) national education systems serve. Discussions are layered and interwoven since the focus on teaching, learning and assessment also requires understanding issues of who, what, why, when and for what purpose. Such questions are also foundational to how feedback is understood and enacted in the spaces between teaching, learning and assessment. Furthermore, these discussions are situated in a complex context in which past, present and future are not easily distinguishable or distinctive. The central issue of feedback in this book is located in a model of formative assessment. This is in a context in which teaching, learning and assessment feature in classrooms on a day-to-day basis. Yet, such interactions cannot be separated from the larger national and international contexts in which they happen. Seeking to explore such interactions more fully is an essential starting point onto which subsequent chapters begin to build and reshape ideas for feedback. Beginning to grasp the possibilities and conditions for different intersections of teaching, learning, and assessment is essential as feedback is further explored in this book as inhabiting these intersecting spaces.

## The importance of teachers

The most fundamental question for our education system that is seldom seriously addressed, is 'What is education for?' The previous chapter sought to give some specific context surrounding why such a question might need to be re-stated. Contemporary national UK educational policy increasingly emphasises the need to raise standards. It centres its narrative on our relative position in international league tables of pupil performance such as the Programme for International Student Assessment (PISA), Trends in International Maths and Science (TiMMS) and Progress in International Reading and Literacy Study (PIRLS), and highlights the importance of education in creating an internationally competitive economy with a skilled workforce. Such an emphasis on the instrumental value of education seems to render primary education as making pupils 'secondary school ready' and secondary education ensuring children are 'work ready'. Furthermore, emphasis on a core of knowledge located mainly within mathematics, English and science adds a particularly narrow focus to what is measured and subsequently what is valued. Although all these are undeniably important, there is little sustained consideration of the experience of education in broader terms.

Issues of difference and diversity, both within and across educational provision, have been challenged. Along with the political steer in schools through the increased powers afforded to the Secretary of State for Education, together with the authority of Ofsted (Office for Standards in Education) to shape schools to deliver exactly what is stated in its inspection framework, conformity has become a significant feature in English schools. As the requirements for demonstrating success have become more precise, visible and incontestable, so the ways in which education is 'produced' has become more unified. As the previous chapter outlined, the impact of high-stakes testing shapes schools in particular ways. Escalating pressure on schools to 'perform' has become overwhelmingly evident through the use of data as a key determinant of national judgements and inspections about school outcomes and success. This shift has been most evident in England since 2010/11 and the introduction of 'RAISEonline' data presentation. This sits alongside the use of Ofsted inspection reports, which graded and publically reported on each school from one (outstanding) to four (categorised as failing). 'RAISEonline' data, now linked to a school data dashboard available online for each school through the Department for Education website, offers an array of data related to a range of variables. This includes segregating data in order to compare outcomes for groups of children, such as children classified as disadvantaged in relation to those who are not, girls and boys, proportions and costs of paid staff, school results related to national averages. Within a grip of accountability, designed to ensure that schools are 'delivering' outcomes in particular ways, the English education system claims that standards are rising and more schools are successful (e.g. Ofsted, 2015: 10).

Any attempt to look beneath the surface is rather more problematic. An initial gaze reveals an education system prioritising core knowledge seen as foundational to children's learning development and providing essential literacy and numeracy for lifelong learning and the world of work. Additionally, such a tight focus provides a context in which teachers are given significant 'status' in ensuring that this happens. In the White Paper *The Importance of Teaching* (DfE, 2010), it was clear that foundational to the aspiration for pupils' learning to be measured and presented in particular ways, was to show standards, and to reveal teachers' competence in delivering these particular requirements. Hence, tighter regulation of teacher training, as well as a shift in who should carry it out, became a further part of national policy directives. Such a policy framework was reinforced in the subsequent White Paper *Educational Excellence Everywhere* (DfE, 2016). Here, not only was the importance of the competence of teachers and the quality of teacher training reasserted, but a much stronger discourse on a notion of equality of outcomes so that 'all' pupils would achieve, and the attainment gap between subsets of pupils reduced. The stated emphasis was clearly on pupil outcomes, but the emphasis shifted between 2010 and 2016, from raising standards, to raising standards for all (DfE, 2016, para 6.1). Further discussion is developed in chapter 4 related to the way in which relationships in classrooms are determined through such a policy discourse. Attention here is more focused on how fundamental notions of teaching, learning and assessment are shaped and influenced.

In essence, the move towards a model of teacher training based predominantly in schools and led by schools (from DfE, 2010) offered a clear way for the tightness of practice emerging in schools to be perpetuated. As schools unified their practices in response to measures of inspection and the importance of published data to determine school success, their distillation of practices to deliver such requirements became the essence of training for the next generation of teachers. Training of teachers thus became a set of standards to be evidenced by the demonstration of prescribed skills, made visible through particular outcomes. This offered a particular pivotal status for teachers, and indeed they are certainly revered in both White Papers (DfE, 2010 and 2016). As Gove (then Secretary of State for Education) declared in the foreword, 'There is no calling more noble, no profession more vital and no service more important than teaching' (DfE, 2010: 7). However, such sentiments offer little to establish their professional knowledge and standing. Furthermore, it may well say more about who will be blamed if standards are not reached.

Underpinning this shift in direction are two further and related developments. Firstly the narrative of 'what works' in education, and secondly the elevated importance of creating an evidence base of teaching. Both of these have developed alongside the changes in education towards a more outcome-related understanding of success. As the outcomes of education became more focused, defined and measured so it became easier to frame 'what works'. In the UK particular attempts have been made to frame 'what works' into specific types of research, and thus construct what is termed an 'evidence base' for education. Papers such as that commissioned by the government from Ben Goldacre (derived from his book: Goldacre, 2009), typify this approach. This is further supported by Haynes et al. (2012) who further present the role of Randomised Controlled Trials (RCTs) as the best method for establishing what works. What this particular construction of an evidence base offers is contentious. In one sense it offers a 'scientific' way to demonstrate which practices offer the best chance of delivering desired outcomes. To some extent there is a logic and coherence to the new emphasis on outcome measures and the robustness of performance being promoted in both policy and practice. However, this form of evidence base fails to share or discuss who or what the evidence base serves. Inherent in the way in which this evidence based model is constructed, and the practices designed to reveal what works, is a lack of consideration of the focus of what works ... for whom, and in what contexts. Such omissions are highly significant, as Biesta (2007) discussed in his critique of the 'what works' approach.

Attempts to make practices in education more robust and evidence based certainly seem to have some appeal. Developments such as Hattie's (2009) 'Visible Learning' in which a meta-analysis has been undertaken across a range of teaching and learning activities in order to identify the 'effect size' of an intervention or aspect of teaching or learning has been well promoted and highly regarded. Hattie's approach offers analysis of aspects of practice supported by information about the amount of evidence available, the cost of the approach and the 'effect size' in terms of additional months of pupil learning gained. The evidence from this work has been complemented and promoted through the Sutton Trust Teaching and Learning Tool Kit. Since 2011, the data considered has also been linked to the Education Endowment Foundation, which was set up by the Department for Education to fund research projects that particularly considered the best practices for the most disadvantaged pupils. Extension of this provision is prioritised in the White Paper (DfE, 2016). Data offered through the format of analysis is intended to be directly useful to schools in ways that can be easily applied in all school contexts.

Such research approaches, although claiming to offer an evidence base that will clarify and improve the relationship between teaching and learning, are deeply problematic. Wiliam gives a clear insight into the difficulties:

> Those who want to determine what works in education are doomed to fail, because in education, 'What works?' is rarely the right question, for the simple reason that in education, just about everything works somewhere, and nothing works everywhere.
>
> *(Wiliam, 2016: 63)*

More specifically, the case of the effective use of teaching assistants (TAs) in class-rooms revealed some of the limitations of the approach used in such meta-analysis. In its early days of offering effect sizes, teaching assistants were given an effect size of zero with some indication that they might even have a negative effect. This caused great concern in schools as the number of teaching assistants had significantly increased since 2000 from 79,000 to 243,700, not to mention the substantial budgetary allocation related to such an increase in numbers. Many of the studies looked more generally at the use of teaching assistants helping lower ability children in whole class contexts. More recent attempts to explore the role and impact of TAs in more nuanced ways revealed a different effect size. When teaching assistants were identified in more targeted and focused roles, working with particular children on targeted interventions in a small group or one-to-one contexts out of the classroom, the effect size was more positive (Sharples et al., 2015). This revealed the importance of both collecting and examining the data in more specific ways. Similar principles may also be the case when feedback is considered. Currently, the effect size for feedback, through the meta-analysis presented through the Education Endowment Foundation, is given as +8 months. Whether this enables us to understand that feedback is effective for all pupils is unclear from this data. This will be explored in more detail in the following chapter and developed throughout this book.

The policy framework prioritising pupil 'outcomes' and a particular notion of establishing and enacting 'what works' offers particular relationships between assessment, teaching and learning. In terms of how the learning gap between what is known and what needs to be known is identified is explored in chapters 4, 5 and 6. How this 'gap' is framed and developed in three different ways is not straightforward. It reflects different approaches to teaching, learning and assessment, which in turn, provide different frameworks in which feedback occurs. It is therefore important to explore in a little more depth the basis upon which teaching, learning and assessment interrelate before they are more specifically examined.

## National policy enactment and the shaping of teaching, learning and assessment relationships

Considerable evidence has emerged in recent years, particularly in the USA, Australia and the UK (Hardy, 2015; Tanner, 2013) concerning how the teaching/learning relationship in classrooms becomes dominated and distorted by the need for particular pupil assessment outcomes. The importance attached to high-stakes assessment renders teaching to be a technically driven operation designed to ensure that pupil outcomes, on the testable curriculum, are as high as they can be. Of particular concern in policy terms is the packaging of the curriculum, the credibility and the use of national (and international) tests reflecting the testable curriculum. This transforms teachers into the agents of delivery of the testable curriculum, and pupils into the outputs, whose 'quality' is determined by the scores they collectively gain in the prioritised testing technologies. Pupils may, therefore, be seen as commodities to indicate a more highly successful economy in an increasingly global marketplace (Pratt, 2016).

Much about the relationship of teaching, learning and assessment is therefore driven by this political agenda and relates to a country's striving agenda to raise its status. Education is seen as a key commodity which highlights increasing success in pupil outcomes as a key indicator of economic success. Echoes of such an agenda were clear in the UK, Australia (Au, 2011; Hardy, 2015) and USA (Tanner, 2013). Such were the concerns of the distortions that national standardised tests had on school practices of teaching and learning that in both the USA and the UK particular changes were introduced aimed at exposing and altering such distortions. There is further discussion in chapter 4 of these issues. Of concern here is how different relationships need to co-exist rather than how one dominates and distorts the others.

In the UK, the final report of the Commission on 'Assessment without Levels' chaired by John McIntosh (DfE, 2015) highlighted how teachers were using data and assessment systems designed for national accountability in order to determine teaching and learning in the classroom. The essence of the report from this commission highlighted the importance of understanding the different purposes of assessment. The national system of levels (set up in 1988) used for accountability at the end of key stages, was also being used by teachers in classrooms for different purposes. The argument offered in the report was constructed around the notion that removing specified levels to which pupils outcomes were judged (in a best fit model) would require schools to design their own assessment systems for classroom based formative assessments. The desired ends of these reforms were for teachers to stop trying to track pupils solely in relation to getting them into the required levels (5). Rather, new approaches to assessment should recognise the importance of developing pupils' depth and breadth of learning, identifying gaps in knowledge that required further attention through teaching.

Significant in these reforms was that the different purposes of assessment should be clearly defined and made distinctive (19). The report outlined three distinct forms of assessment: day-to-day in-school formative assessment; in-school summative assessment, and nationally standardised summative assessments. Recognising these distinctions, each with different purposes, was key to shifting away from the more distorting practices of national summative assessments on teaching and learning. At the heart of these UK changes in 2014–2016 was a renewed emphasis on teachers' skills, understanding and actions in assessing within everyday classroom contexts. Here, specific boundaries were being re-established so that both purpose and practice between standardised assessments for accountability and teacher assessments were more clearly demarcated.

## Re-establishing the distinctiveness of formative assessment

Formative assessment is certainly not a new notion. Conceptually it draws its provenance from Scriven (1967), who drew a distinction between formative and summative assessments at a programme level. He distinguished programme evaluations that were designed to indicate overall judgements of programme success (summative) from programme evaluations that were designed to help improve programmes (formative). It was Bloom (1969: 48) who shifted the focus of formative evaluation to formative assessment, related to pupil assessment. He described its purpose as being 'to provide feedback and correctives at each stage in the teaching-learning processes'. Sadler (1989) made a distinctive contribution in suggesting that formative assessment was linked to providing and acting on information that altered the gap between what a pupil currently knows and needs to know next. Conceptualisation of formative assessment was rather more evident than its practical application for many decades.

In the UK, it was the launch of the Task Group for Assessment and Testing (DFES, TGAT: 1988), set up as part of the development of the National

Curriculum in 1988, which contributed to assessment being brought centre stage. The particular focus here was to construct a national assessment process that would serve the new curriculum. In so doing it sought to incorporate formative, summative, evaluative and diagnostic assessment (Department for Education and Science, Task group on Assessment and Testing, 1988, para 23). However, there was a clear view that 'an assessment system designed for formative assessment can meet all the needs of national assessment at ages before 16' (para 26). At the time this seemed to be a favourable approach, as concerns had been raised that standard assessments were driving educational reform processes (Haviland, 1988; Murphy, 1987). It offered assurances that teacher involvement linked to formative assessment would be central in the age phases spanning 5–16. However, as Black and Wiliam (2003) outlined over the following decade, 'the idea that National Curriculum assessment should support the formative purpose has been all but ignored' (625). More significantly, perhaps within the decade, there was a shift in the idea that formative assessment by teachers (Teacher Assessment) should feed into summative assessment, diminished. The legacy of this shift may not only be just that summative national assessments reign supreme, but that teachers' understanding and practice of formative assessment has also been diminished and distorted, as the systems to support it have been largely ignored.

The removal of National Curriculum assessment levels in England (DfE, 2015) was therefore particularly significant. It reopened the possibility for a system-level acceptance of the importance of teachers developing their skills and tools for formative assessment. It enabled a return to some of the issues and principles that formative assessment could develop. As Black and Wiliam set out in their research (1998b and 1998c), formative assessment had the potential to raise standards but it was not a simple matter with no easy quick fixes (1998c: 15). What they did clarify was that it encompassed activities by both teachers and pupils, which generated data that, through the focus of feedback, could subsequently influence both teaching and learning (1998b: 7–8). Feedback thus becomes located centrally in formative assessment practices.

Understanding formative assessment is necessary from several perspectives. First, at a system level, which, as illustrated above, positions it in relation to teaching and learning as well as against other forms of assessment. Second, conceptually, in terms of the underpinnings that pervade the formation and construction of the third and fourth perspectives of 'process' and 'method'. At a fundamental level of understanding, it must be remembered that in addition to being a process that enables more effective teaching and learning, it is an assessment approach. It therefore requires judgement and decision making. What makes formative assessment distinctive is that the decisions and judgements made are intended to influence teaching and learning to bring about adaptations to both. Critically, issues related to validity and reliability are very different. What is particularly significant in this book is how both teachers AND pupils need to be part of the formative assessment process in an active way so that both may adapt together for greater synergy between teaching and learning.

This offers a very particular conceptual perspective which pervades the way in which teaching and learning co-exist, and which formative assessment serves.

Central to this co-existent relationship between teaching and learning within formative assessment, is feedback. Its contextualising as a process within formative assessment and between teaching and learning is important to further clarify in this chapter.

## Formative assessment, assessment *for* learning and assessment *as* learning

Central to understanding formative assessment are the processes and techniques involved. Bennett (2011: 6) makes it clear that early definitions of formative assessment tended to view it as either a process or a method (or instrument). The distinction is often exacerbated by test publishers promoting formative assessment in terms of particular marketed instruments that would serve specified diagnostic purposes. Researchers and educators often sat on the 'process' side of the debate emphasising the importance of assessment that served a formative purpose, permitting teachers to adapt their teaching to develop pupil learning. In an attempt to dodge some of the definitional difficulties, Bennett highlights that the two need to be synthesised, and that 'strong conceptualisation needs to give careful attention to each component. As well as to how the two components work together to provide useful feedback' (7).

In the UK the term Assessment for Learning (AfL) was developed following the Assessment Reform Group's (1999) framing of assessment as being designed to 'promote learning' (6). It was characterised by the following:

• it is embedded in a view of teaching and learning of which it is an essential part;
• it involves sharing learning goals with pupils;
• it aims to help pupils to know and to recognise the standards they are aiming for;
• it involves pupils in self-assessment;
• it provides feedback which leads to pupils recognising their next steps and how to take them;
• it is underpinned by confidence that every student can improve;
• it involves both teacher and pupils reviewing and reflecting on assessment data.

*(The Assessment Reform Group, 1999: 7)*

This offered a slightly different perspective from the original discussion defining formative assessment, which was more specifically framed as leading to adapting teaching in the classroom. This shift in focus, to embrace learning, offered a different priority. Furthermore, it drew attention not only to the teachers but to the pupils. Rather than just helping the teacher to refine and change teaching to be more effective, it recognised that ultimately formative assessment is about learning. It is the pupils who learn. Thus, in exploring both the processes and instruments for AfL, consideration needs to be given to both the teachers and the pupils as participants in the teaching/learning encounter. It requires both to be active in this educational encounter. With such a stance, AfL becomes less of a technical assessment mechanism, providing data easily translated into specific teaching techniques. Rather, it becomes part of an educational experience in which learning advances. Learning needs to be more specially focused in the context of AfL so that smaller steps can be outlined from day to day rather than at the end of a phase of study.

In this book, particular attention is given to the relationship between teaching and learning through the process of assessment. More specifically, it examines how feedback processes between the teacher and pupil do and might influence both teaching and learning. With such a focus, both the conceptual framing and the possible processes are not straightforward. They are not simply technically framed so that they can be easily scaled up and implemented, although it is hoped that relevant and adaptable insights and possibilities can be shared. They are founded on relational experiences within an educational process (this is developed further in chapter 5). As such, they are complex, interpersonal and embedded.

## Pupil positioning

Although the arguments and discussions in the book are built within notions of AfL, there is a far more specific positioning. This relates to my previous work on assessment *as* learning (AaL) (Dann, 2002 and 2014). 'AaL is the complex interplay of assessment, teaching and learning which holds at its core the notion that pupils must understand their own learning progress and goals through a range of processes which are themselves cognitive events' (2014: 150–151). What is therefore promoted is that the pupils' role is central to the process of 'assessment as learning' to the extent that assessment becomes part of the learning process. The information yielded from AfL thus reveals insights about learning for the individual learner which become part of the process of learning. This shifts learning away from being merely a technical process of content knowledge to a more complex interplay of content, context, persons and process. The fundamental premise for this book rests on my previous assertion,

> Pupils need to understand something of the gap between where they are in their learning and where they might be. Although a next step of learning may be teacher constructed or nationally prescribed, if it is not grasped by the pupil as an aspiration, next step, target or goal, then it is unlikely to be realised.
>
> *(Dann, 2002: 111)*

What becomes evident within this context is that the relationships between teaching, learning and assessment are not simple and linear. So too, the positioning of teachers, learners and the curriculum becomes mediated through assessment processes. These become necessarily inter-personal and reciprocal. Feedback has the potential to become the mediating tool that weaves in and through the processes of teaching and learning, serving both teaching (and teachers) and learning (and learners). Further exploration of feedback forms the focus of the following chapter (3). This chapter continues to examine the relationship of teaching, learning and assessment. Attention is next turned to socio-cultural theories that are foundational to the participatory and situated notions underpinning AfI and AaL in this book.

## Socio-cultural historical activity theory underpinnings

Essential to the way in which AfI and AaL are understood and promoted in this book are the ways in which people and context are understood and inter-relate. As alluded to in the previous chapter, learning within national (and international) policy seems to be commodified. Here, learning is broadened and takes further account of Biesta's (2006, 2010) notion of learning as part of an experience of education. Socio-cultural theory is at the core of this book. It recognises that learning is not a one-way transmission process where knowledge is given to pupils. Rather, it recognises that education is participatory (all participants are active), and that actions are situated in particular contexts. These contexts relate to the past, the present and the future. Dewey (1929) emphasises that communication is the foundational basis for education. He conceives communication 'as the establish-ment of cooperation in an activity in which there are partners, and in which the activity of each is modified and regulated by partnership. To fail to understand is to fail to come to agreement in action' (179). Education is therefore, framed as par-ticipatory, and linked to exploring common meanings through communication. Feedback can be seen as an essential tool here. For Dewey, education is not exclusively about either teaching or learning but the communicative participatory space between the two.

The notions of participation and activity are central to cultural historical activity theory (CHAT). As Crossouard (2009) highlights, CHAT offers greater potential for embracing different identities, tensions, discourses and conflicts than social cultural theory alone. Socio-cultural theory emphasises the social nature of constructed knowledge and meaning with less emphasis on the different layers of activity that an individual may bring to any encounter. This is discussed more fully in relation to AaL in Dann (2014). However, a particular premise promoted in this book is that ALL participants in the educational encounter will have different perspectives, identities, roles and interpretations. Even though there are different power and responsibility positions at stake within the teacher and pupil encounter, there must be recognition that each will necessarily bring more than the content of learning. Reducing each participant into a tightly focused knowledge-centred encounter is unlikely to represent the realities of either teaching or learning. As the research in chapter 7, as well as Dann (2015) highlights, some of the presumptions about what children think and how they respond to the instructions and priorities of teachers, may be naively underconsidered in our classrooms.

The more central role of learners, as active participants with their own lives, past, present and future, is a key contribution that this book brings to discussions about the interfacing of teaching, learning and assessment. As part of a socio-cultural theoretical positioning there are particular notions of past, present and future that are important in understanding teaching, learning and assessment which require some consideration here.

## Past, present and future

In 1911 Edmond Holmes controversially challenged the prevailing educational regime, overshadowed by the policy of 'Payments by Results', with his plea for a very different way of thinking about education. He was an articulate critic of the use of examinations to measure student outcomes for accountability purposes, as the following brief extracts exemplify.

> My aim, in writing this book, is to show that the externalism of the West, the prevalent tendency to pay undue regard to outward and visible 'results' and to neglect what is inward and vital, is the source of most of the defects that vitiate Education in this country, and therefore that the only remedy for those defects is the drastic one of changing our standard of reality and our conception of the meaning and value of life.
>
> *(Holmes, 1911, Preface, vi)*

> In a school which is ridden by the examination incubus, the whole atmosphere is charged with deceit. The teacher's attempt to outwit the examiner is deceitful; and the immorality of his action is aggravated by the fact that he makes his pupils partners with him in his fraud.
>
> *(65)*

His optimism pointed to a different way of looking towards the future for the education of children rather than continually seeking to locate pupil success in specific ways related to the past. This offered a very particular understanding of different purposes of assessment and recognised that life not learning should be part of what education outcomes should be about. But clearly such a broad remit would fall foul of any robust validity and testing framework so highly regarded. His criticisms of the impact of testing were not too far removed from current challenges to national testing in the first two decades of the twenty-first century. As Richards (2010) contends, Holmes' writing is still as relevant. Yet building on Holmes' turn of phrase 'what is and what might be', has been a popular statement for those seeking to look differently on what and how education might be. It looks to a future rather than being focused on the past. More specifically, it looks beyond assessment which only examines what has been learnt and shifts attention towards ways of optimising how assessment might help to support what might be learnt in the future. This is a very significant shift, not only in assessment, but in the purpose of education. In some senses, as soon as the focus of education becomes focused on the future, all participants become more equal, as no one has control of an unknown future. Yielding power over what 'might be' is less clear-cut than determining status over what has been.

Within national policy, considerable attention is given to establishing policy based on past notions of excellence, which recognises achievement in a context of what has previously been given particular status. The present, in terms of education policy, is therefore, often precariously founded on a particular version of the past, that is directed towards a very specific economically framed future. In terms of the national curriculum and assessment in England, this seems to be the case. It is focused on a notion of pupil achievement, based on testable school knowledge, shaping the future prosperity and competitiveness of the country. The school experience for pupils is very much based on acquiring the pre-defined knowledge, set out in the core subjects of the national curriculum, which will serve the future of the country. To some extent there seems to be an idealisation of the past through the curriculum and an optimism for a future economy. The present, the here and now, for children living and learning today, is not of much concern in policy terms in England.

Such a view poses an important area of consideration. If national policy offers the connections between the past, present and future in the way described, assessment is focused on the achievement and success of particular knowledge. Teachers therefore focus on teaching and assessing such knowledge, and the use of feedback becomes almost exclusively directed towards these ends. Formative assessment, however, is about future learning. It can, of course, be mainly directed towards helping pupils to gain the knowledge which will be tested in summative assessments. However, as it is about future learning, it is thus future-orientated. Inherent within it is the scope for new learning and experience for both teachers and pupils. The key question here is whether the dominant discourse of a national curriculum which is taught and measured through a required set of expected outcomes, can be both imagined and experienced through a different formation of past, present and future.

Klenowski and Wyatt-Smith (2014) point to the idea of futures-orientated assessment. In their vision, knowledge is conceived 'as knowledge creation and development of new materials and conceptual artefacts' (157–8). Although located in the present, through participant learning communities, the emphasis lies beyond to the notion of participatory co-construction. The 'trialogical' approach is drawn from Paavola and Hakkarainen (2005) and emphasises that interaction is through common objects (artefacts) of activity. It thus lies not only in social constructivism but in the cultural historical activity theory (CHAT) already highlighted in this chapter. It therefore brings together the social, the active and the object orientation. Furthermore, it offers the possibilities for different knowledge creations, rather than merely a replication of what has come before. This provides a very different outlook when educational policy seeks to predetermine outcomes in relation to particular predetermined performance standards.

There is considerable tension in education over whether children should be taught a basic knowledge content prior to being given more flexible and creative opportunities. To what extent can children embrace the creative, without a foundation of knowledge on which such creativity and knowledge creation can be founded? The longstanding debate, often framed as polar opposites between a traditional and progressive educational approach, is often unhelpful in seeking to establish appropriate understanding. An enduring and repeated problem within these debates is that they become superficial, and some of the thinking and philosophical reasoning that underpinned them is lost.

A particularly poignant and relevant example in recent education debates, which are foundational in both the UK and USA, relates to E.D. Hirsch's (2006) ideas surrounding knowledge deficit and constructing a common core knowledge within a national curriculum. E.D. Hirsch is typically known for promoting the idea of a nationally agreed core curriculum. Indeed, in the UK, in 2015, the Secretary and Minister of States for Education Nick Gibbs and Michael Gove (respectively), openly discussed the influence of Hirsch's ideas on the reframing and updating of the National Curriculum in England (Gibbs, 2015). It thus sits pivotally in contemporary discussion of the relationship of teaching and learning. Gove, in a key speech in 2009, focused on what education is for from a Hirschian perspective and stated:

> A society in which there is a widespread understanding of the nation's past, a shared appreciation of cultural reference points, a common stock of knowledge on which all can draw, and trade, is a society in which we all understand each other better, one in which the ties that bind are stronger, and more resilient at times of strain.
>
> *(Gibbs, 2015: 13)*

From this starting point, he promised to 'completely overhaul the curriculum – to ensure that the acquisition of knowledge within rigorous subject disciplines is properly valued and cherished' (13). This became the foundation for the revised National Curriculum in England in 2013. What seemed apparent here was that the conceptualising of the curriculum was about acquiring selected structured and planned knowledge from the past. The purpose, seemingly, was to agree and construct common ground, which would help relationships between citizens when they were potentially strained.

There are some interesting twists here in relation to the ideas which Hirsch promotes. Part of Hirsch's original intentions was to address the difficulties that certain more disadvantaged children experienced as they started school with less 'cultural literacy' than other children (Hirsch, 2006). From this starting point (in America) the education system was merely widening this already existing gap, thus creating a 'knowledge deficit'. All important for Hirsch, in his vision for improving American schooling, was the importance of an education that would enable children to learn new things for themselves. Reading was considered the key to learning. This was not merely about the skills of decoding (which need initially to be learnt), rather 'it's what reading enables you to do that is critical. In the information age, the key to economic and policy achievement is the ability to gain new knowledge rapidly through reading and listening' (2006: 2). For Hirsch, the key to being able to read in a way that enables new learning, is through having good background knowledge so that information can be comprehended. It is the ability to comprehend that is key to Hirsch's ideas. This, he claims, is best promoted not only through trying to teach reading or comprehension skills, but by teaching broad enabling knowledge, through a knowledge-orientated reading programme (17). For Hirsch, formal teaching in the basics of reading, grammar, vocabulary knowledge and speaking are essential, so too is a carefully constructed knowledge-oriented curriculum. Certainly, the national curriculum and its associated testing (in England) serve the first three of these aims. It does so to the extent that, as previously discussed, it seems to distort the whole curriculum. Thus, the claims by Gove and Gibbs that the Hirschian model has been developed and embedded into the schooling system of England might be supported.

Furthermore, through additional funding for children from more disadvantaged families (Pupil Premium) additional support is available for these children. From Hirsch's perspective, these children often have more limited cultural literacy and more limited vocabularies so do not learn as quickly as other children. The 'Pupil Premium' is therefore designed to fund experiences in school that are planned to give further support for these children. Even though every school in England must publish on its website what this money is used for and the impact it has for the children it is designed to serve, there is little consensus over what 'works'. But what seems at odds with Hirsch's thinking is that he claims that the greatest benefit for these children is to increase the breadth of their vocabulary from an early age, which he claims, will ultimately give them the cultural literacy they need. He discusses the best approach to such an endeavour as being through 'indirect, implicit learning' (62). However, he does acknowledge that discrete and explicit learning of vocabulary has some effect. Here, Hirsch teases out the longstanding debate over traditional and progressive approaches. He discusses formal explicit teaching as well as more 'natural' approaches. Whereas, at times he criticises the more romantic progressive notions of teaching, he does concede at this point that when the focus is on enhancing vocabulary as early as possible in children's lives, implicit methods that recognise a child's interest and experiences are of greater value. Hirsch recognises 'naturalism in learning is not always wrong, it appears. It depends on what is to be learnt' (63). Thus, he suggests that an approach to tackling the knowledge deficit in America requires an explicitly taught, structured knowledge curriculum which sits alongside the importance of developing each individual child's vocabulary in relation to each child's own experiences.

Therefore, oversimplification of Hirsch's ideas and their reduction to a set of knowledge which marginalises a child's own interests and renders successes only in terms of outcomes of remembered knowledge is a far cry from what Hirsch outlines. The desired outcomes for Hirsch may in some terms be reflected in ensuring that children have basic structured knowledge, particularly in reading. (He also mentions the importance of mathematics.) Measuring school success in terms of outcomes and standards is certainly identifiable as a Hirschian strand. Yet, to focus so strongly on such specific testable knowledge, as defined by English Education policy (DfE, 2010 and 2016) and the outcome-driven inspection framework in England, is an extremely limited and even damaging interpretation.

If education is about helping pupils to learn for themselves and equipping them with the knowledge and the skills to derive meaning and new learning from what they read, then education has an important 'present' that needs to be monitored, accounted for, and serve its participants well. However, it is designed for a future of new possibilities and new horizons for each learner. Simple testable measurable outcomes seem less valuable here.

This notion of learning being about a new future and AfL leading the pathway for this future is seldom explored with the attention it deserves. Part of this future may well be known, planned and part of national government policy for expected standards. However, no matter how determined and regulated part of the future of each child may be, every child's learning future will be unique. Ultimately, such futures are just a part of our 'human condition' and as such are essentially unique (Arendt, 1958). Just as Hirsch identified a notion of cultural literacy with which a child engages with what school has to offer, this is just a part of a broader sense of being literate for learning. What I mean here is not merely about literacy in a language-orientated way, but rather the ability to engage, combine and make sense of layers of activity and participation in life, of which school learning is just a part. Navigating such futures is a pathway that each pupil must tread. School experiences and pedagogic design can only lay out pathways, direct travel and help reinforce thinking steps along the way. It can set out what needs to be remembered and give spaces and strategies for such remembering. It can signpost and push what is important and try to ensure its visibility amidst the plethora of bombarding and competing components of a child's life. Part of what this book begins to develop is how the relationship of teaching, learning and assessment may serve society and pupils better. More importantly, it considers how to construct, support, rescue and direct a communicative journey towards new learnings – expected and unexpected ones. The role of feedback seems an important mediating tool in this process. To date, feedback has not been sufficiently understood, developed or applied for the role that it could and should play in a school system that seeks new futures (personal, social and economic).

The following chapter examines feedback in the context of existing research evidence and points to opportunities for different positionings and understandings that are subsequently explored in this book.

# 3

# WHAT DO WE KNOW ABOUT FEEDBACK?

## Chapter overview

This chapter is aimed at highlighting significant issues related to our understanding and enactment of feedback. It explores key issues that have prevailed in research studies on the definitions, frequency, purpose, form and focus of feedback. The chapter is not intended to offer a new systematic review or new synthesis of research evidence. Rather, it is intended to distil key themes, and tease out why there are so many contradictions and confusions inherent in the available research. It offers challenge and critique to some of the prevailing notions, particularly to the dominant discourse of determining notions of feedback effectiveness through meta-analysis, using only quantitatively structured types of research. The way in which feedback is interpreted by all participants, in specific contexts, is given particular attention. The chapter considers issues of validity as an important dimension to understanding what feedback is for, who it serves and whether its consequences matter. Illuminating some of the limitations of our understanding and conceptualising of feedback from the existing literature at the end of this chapter, offers a context for the remainder of the book. The chapter establishes feedback as a relational concept based on communicative action and interaction.

## The research field on feedback

> Few concepts have been written about more uncritically and incorrectly than that of feedback.
>
> *(Latham and Locke, 1991: 224)*

Feedback is centre stage in educational arenas in which there are ever increasing pressures for performance outcomes to rise. The reason for this relates to the high status given to attempts to reveal 'what works' for raising outcomes, evidenced through 'effect size' data derived from meta-analyses. In England, the Sutton Trust Tool Kit along with the government-funded Educational Endowment Foundation (Teaching and Learning Tool Kit) offer a range of evidence that is aimed at presenting information about strategies and interventions that are most effective. Feedback is evidenced in this data as having a particularly high 'effect size' (+8, signifying gains equivalent to more than 8 months). It, along with 'metacognition and self-regulation', has the highest effect size of all strategies reported (Education Endowment Foundation, 2016). However, on further inspection, additional information is offered which indicates that more recent studies report more modest impact, and that making feedback work is challenging. What becomes very quickly apparent to anyone who seeks to understand feedback is that it is complex both conceptually and pragmatically. Evidence ranges considerably from feedback having a positive effect to, in Kluger and DeNisi's (1996) research, a third of studies reporting a negative effect. Research findings on feedback are certainly 'highly variable' (Kluger and DeNisi, 1998: 254) or even 'conflicting' (Shute 2008: 153). This baffling state of affairs seems to have triggered a range of systematic reviews, further research studies and further meta-analysis. The outcomes of such endeavours do not seem to have moved us closer to better understanding the effectiveness of feedback in improving learning.

There seem to be two key factors that are deeply problematic, and greatly contribute to the uncertainties in understanding, developing and using feedback. The first relates to the dominant approach through which 'what works' is explored and determined. The second links to the way in which feedback is conceptualised and enacted. This is considered later in this chapter. The first is briefly discussed in the following section.

## Meta-analysis in research on feedback

Much of the argument created around the effectiveness of feedback has been drawn from meta-analysis. This is a statistically based process drawing together the results from many studies in order to synthesise an 'effect size'. Combining studies is thought to allow a greater evidence base for the effects of research. Even though evidence about feedback has been based on meta-analysis, it is clear that this basis is highly problematic. Even those who have quoted the statistics from it to promote the impact of feedback within formative assessment have also criticised its limitations. Notably, Black and Wiliam (1998a: 53), in their high-profile review of formative assessment, highlight how problematic the process of meta-analysis is for establishing anything meaningful. More recently, Wiliam (2016: 115) very clearly explains that giving any credence to these effect size claims 'may have been a mistake'. Such comments have further contributed to what Bennett (2011: 12) identifies as the 'urban legend' of the effectiveness of formative assessment and particularly feedback.

Wiliam (2016) explores in more depth what the 'effect size' from meta-analysis data offers. Feedback is used as the prime example of how the process of meta-analysis reduces the meaningfulness of what is being researched throughout the process. He gives an example of a meta-analysis in the area of feedback, where there were initially 9,000 published papers on the effectiveness of feedback in mathematics, science and technology. These were reduced to 238 papers and then to 111 which were considered to have sufficient quantitative data to reveal the impact of feedback on student achievement (60 in mathematics, 35 in science and 16 in technology). Of the studies remaining, 85 per cent identified feedback as a singular event lasting just a few minutes, and most pupils had not been told what the feedback was for. The point Wiliam diligently seeks to make is that the outcomes of such a meta-analysis are likely to be of very little use when applied in an educational context. He concludes that the results of meta-analysis 'will be at best meaningless and at worst misleading' (96).

Bennett (2011) argues in a similar vein, yet despite such caution and even criticism, in England the importance of research based on quantitative data that is combined through meta-analysis is strongly promoted. It seems to be regarded as a good basis for an evidence-based profession seeking to establish and disseminate 'what works' (DfE, 2016). The statistical facade behind which dubious data is scaffolded is highly puzzling. If feedback has an effect size of between 0.4 and 0.7/0.8 (Black and Wiliam 1998c; Hattie, 2009; Shute 2008) then we are still not sure whether these possible gains are part of what is normally expected or are additional. If they are additional and gained incrementally year on year, then the impact and cost efficiencies for our education system would be phenomenal (Wiliam, 2016). Furthermore, it is clear from the statistical trends on pupil performance across the age range in England, that such gains are not being achieved. Possible deductions here, claims Wiliam, are that either the meta-analysis is inaccurate and misleading, or that teachers are not sufficiently enacting the research evidence available to make full use of the possible benefits of the research evidence.

The key message here is that claims made about feedback might not be what they seem when related solely to accumulated quantitative statistical data. The wide-ranging findings about the effectiveness of feedback reveal more about its complexity than about finding simple solutions to establishing 'what works'. What is of greater benefit is to seek out what we can understand about feedback from the wider research field. A number of published review papers have charted some of the research territory in relation to formative assessment and particularly feedback (Bennett, 2011; Black and Wiliam, 1998; Hattie and Timperley 2007; Heitink et al., 2016; Shute, 2008; Butler and Winne, 1995). In setting out key parameters for our understanding of feedback, the next section teases out some of the key research findings that help to frame feedback. The next section is not intended to be an additional contribution to systemic review. Rather, it attempts to present some of the ways in which research has tried to construct and capture the enactment of feedback. It is not intended to be exhaustive but representative of the field.

## Framing definitions of feedback

The term feedback is in common usage and can transverse many disciplines and contexts. It is recognised in everyday discourses in management, ecology, biology, acoustics, as well as education. In its very broadest sense, feedback is 'something' (information, chemical, biological, electrical) that has been received which can subsequently be used for/or causes change within a cycle, gap or system. As Ramaprasad (1983: 4), reinforced subsequently by Sadler (1989: 121), states 'it is information about the gap between the actual level and the reference level of a system parameter which is used to alter the gap in some way'. Within this very broad framing of the term, there is an expectation that the information does something to an existing state to alter it. Hence, it must be sufficiently specific so that it can direct such change or alteration. However, the resulting change or alteration may be for better or worse and may not be as intended. Hence, feedback discourses include notions of positive and negative feedback outcomes and are not always predictable.

Within education, feedback can be at a system, group or individual level. Hattie and Timperley (2007: 81) in their systematic review, state their conceptualisation of feedback as 'information provided by an agent (e.g. teacher, peer, book, parent, self, experience) regarding an aspect of one's performance or understanding'. They declare that it is a 'consequence of performance'. Some of the derivations for this view stem from early behaviourist theory in which feedback is regarded as information that will reinforce behaviour in order to influence whether certain behaviours or responses should be repeated, adjusted or ceased (Thorndike, 1913; Skinner, 1954). Thus, although feedback is designed to influence future behaviour it is separate from such behaviour. What is therefore less clear from such definitions, is whether feedback is merely information or whether it must have gained a response for it to be considered as feedback.

Black and Wiliam (1998a: 53) state that 'for the sake of simplicity, the term feedback should be used in its least restrictive sense, to refer to any information that is provided to the performer of any action about that performance'. However, for it to be formative, they claim, it must also address a shift in the learning gap. Shute (2008: 154) defines formative feedback 'as information communicated to the learner that is intended to modify his or her thinking or behaviour for the purpose of improving learning'. This shifts the definition from information as data to information with specific intentions.

Within the Higher Education (HE) context, feedback is typically regarded as the information provided by academics to students (Boud and Molloy, 2013). Indeed, institutions are judged through student satisfaction surveys on student perceptions which include students' views on the quality of the feedback they receive. Thus, it seems that particular prominence is given to the way lecturers can 'better dangle the data' in the form of feedback for students (699). Improvements in feedback practices are very much located within the grasp of the institution, the tutors and the lecturers. However, research in the HE context has certainly recognised the significance of student perceptions and enactment. For feedback to shift the learning gap, it requires students to adjust their learning. It therefore requires understanding of the ways in which students act on the feedback.

Discussion is further located within the notion of sustainable feedback (Carless et al., 2011). In the HE context, the ability of students to be self-regulated and be able to take control of their own learning, consciously using feedback in this process, is far less problematic (theoretically and developmentally) than it might be for school-aged children. With particular assumptions about learning, the use of feedback can be understood and developed with students in ways that might lead to more sustainable learner practices. As Boud and Molloy (2013) argue, feedback should be designed to increasingly lead the student to require less externally given feedback, as they seek out their own feedback, becoming their own 'elicitors of knowledge improvement' (705).

The arguments in HE have moved on further than those typically rehearsed in school contexts. There is more research linked to student perceptions, understandings and use of feedback. Adcroft (2011) firmly locates feedback as a social process and particularly lays bare what he terms 'the mythology of feedback'. Here the importance of recognising other 'mythological lenses' is important (Macdonald et al., 2006: 28). In the context of feedback, a recipient of feedback may have particular cultural priorities, beliefs and prior learning which may lead to different ways of understanding and acting on feedback than those intended by the person offering the feedback. Thus, recognising the 'dissonance' that such difference may create is important. Adcroft further highlights that such dissonance also requires the 'social process of *commensuration*, whereby common ground is found' (2011: 406).

Such discussions from the HE sector are less well defined within research on pupil feedback within schools. Children, whose learning skills are considered less developed, are more tentatively considered in relation to self-regulatory mechanisms. However, feedback as part of a self-regulatory process is a very clear strand in the research on feedback. It is considered later in this chapter. What is less explicit when feedback is considered with children, are the notions of sustainability of learning (how they can increasingly sustain their own learning) and how 'dissonance' and subsequently 'commensuration' might be recognised. Part of the contribution of this book is the recognition that even at a young age, teaching and learning need to be pointing towards an ultimate desire for learning to become sustainable and that learner perceptions of themselves will influence the ways in which they seek out and use feedback at all stages. Trying to understand this in more nuanced ways, so that feedback is neither seen simply as a technique to be refined by teachers and/or school systems, nor as merely a self-regulatory mechanism, is the essence of the argument developed in this book.

Certainly, Hattie and Timperley also identify that feedback occurs in a context and has 'no effect in a vacuum' (2007: 82). Layered within this latter view is another crucial dimension. Bennett (2011: 14) draws attention to this in his consideration of formative assessment. He claims feedback is partly a matter of inference. Who is making inferences, and on what basis they are made, is all important.

Perceptions of context and evidence thus become more complex. What is less clear in much of the literature is how the context influences the feedback, and the meanings and inferences drawn in both giving and receiving feedback. Indeed, in much of the literature, the immediate context in which the feedback is given is suspended in order to isolate feedback processes and techniques. However, the view in this book is that context is integral when feedback is considered within formative assessment.

Within the developing literature, formative feedback is identified as a key component of formative assessment or AfL (Black and Wiliam, 2009; Nicol and Macfarlane-Dick, 2006; Assessment Reform Group, 2002). Indeed, Black and Wiliam (1998a: 36) claim that quality feedback is the 'key feature' for effective formative assessment. With the increased status and role of formative assessment receiving attention, understanding and using feedback are therefore crucial. It may well be that this positioning, within an assessment framework, has resulted in the type of research and perspective that prevails in the literature. The important point revealed here is that feedback can be understood differently depending on the conceptual as well as the physical context in which it is explored. Askew and Lodge (2000) illustrated this well in locating feedback quite differently according to the dominant learning theory adopted (feedback as a 'gift', feedback as 'ping-pong', feedback as 'loops', pp. 5–16). This link with learning theory is further extended in the literature so that it is not only part of the chosen theoretical discourse offered by teachers, but also an aspect of the learning repertoire used by learners. Thus, as well as being seen as a tool for assessment, it can also be seen as a mediating process for learning, and seen in more psychological terms in connection with processes of self-regulation (Butler and Winne, 1995; Nicol and Macfarlane-Dick, 2006) and motivation (Dweck 1986). Such multiplicity of approaches and perspectives adds to the richness of the concept, but renders it more difficult to simplify.

Following Ramaprasad (1983) and Sadler's (1989) insights, feedback is a mechanism which is designed to reduce the gap between what is not known and what is known. The context here is bound by particular notions of what is to be learnt and what is already known. Any notion of effectiveness for feedback is therefore connected with 'altering the gap'. Much of the understanding contained in this view has been connected with teachers making an assessment judgement about what is known, and identifying what is needed to be known next, while seeking to communicate this. To some extent teaching can even be seen as a form of feedback if it has been structured and planned in response to the learning needs of the pupils. In this context it becomes the means of teachers controlling, defining and shaping the learning gap for children. Hattie and Timperley (2007: 82) draw attention to this notion as the process of feedback is translated into the next instruction. This may be more akin to the reflective process for the teacher, and is not typically the way in which research on feedback is explored.

The focus, which is of greater concern, is how feedback is in some way a form of communication with pupils about how their learning might progress. This is a key contribution of this book. Implicit again is the notion of a learning gap, and that feedback is the tool for identifying what needs to be done to bridge the gap. Two clear strands become apparent in making sense of feedback from this perspective. First, what are the best ways to communicate gap-closing information (constructing feedback) and what do learners need to do in their response to it (receiving feedback)? Both of these will be briefly explored. It is worth noting that the assumption here is that the gap that needs to be closed (or altered) is very much regarded as being in the control of the teacher. Whether it is understood or valued by the pupil is a very different question, which will be explored later.

## Constructing feedback

There has been much research that has sought to portray the best type of feedback for altering the learning gap. Matters for consideration have included when feedback should be given, how often, what purpose it should serve, and what its form and focus should be. It is not intended to convey all the research evidence here, as detailed papers already serve this purpose (such as Hattie and Timperley, 2007; Shute, 2008). The aim here is to identify some of the parameters for consideration that can usefully shape feedback.

## Frequency and timing of feedback

Of particular concern here relates to whether the frequency of the feedback makes a difference as well as whether it is best given immediately or after a time has elapsed. Shute (2008) indicates that the research about the timing of feedback yields inconsistent findings. The issues of whether feedback is given immediately or delayed yield different and even conflicting findings. Overall, the conclusion is that delayed feedback may slow the rate of initial learning, but help to transfer learning in the longer term. Immediate feedback helps to correct errors so that the errors are not remembered. However, in addition to this generalisation, research by Hattie and Timperley (2007) and Shute (2008) has also suggested that the timing of feedback is related to the nature of the task and the capability of the learner. Shute reports that immediate feedback is more effective when the task is difficult, whereas if the task is easy then delayed feedback is preferable. However, it should also be noted that if the tasks are too easy or too difficult motivation and engagement levels change which may make any feedback less effective.

## The purpose and focus of feedback

From the definitions already offered, feedback (that is formative) should alter a learning gap in some way in education. However, this can be achieved in more than one way. Black and Wiliam (1998a) identify two main purposes of feedback: directive and facilitative. These relate firstly to focusing on what needs to be corrected (directive) and secondly, on helping pupils in their own process of change (facilitative). Very clearly there are distinctions here in terms of the focus. Firstly, the emphasis is on the correctness of the learning in terms of tasks, goals or outcomes. Secondly, there is an emphasis on the process of pupil learning through their own understanding of their next steps and through self-regulation. Kulhavy and Stock (1989) had previously highlighted a distinction between feedback that offered 'verification' as compared to 'elaboration'. In a similar vein differences between feedback that seek to verify answers (as correct or incorrect) offers a more explicit approach. Elaboration can be focused and direct, but can also be more facilitative. Torrance and Pryor (1998: 153–154) and Pryor and Crossouard (2008), for example, highlight 'divergent' and 'convergent' approaches to feedback. Convergent assessment includes information related to a correct response and is focused on the task to be completed (2008: 4). Divergent feedback, in contrast, is identified as 'exploratory, provisional and provocative' (2008: 4).

There are some slight differences in the language used in the distinctions offered in these definitions. The terms 'directive', 'verification' and 'convergent' give specific focus on correctness and clear focus in relation to something specific, and whether or not it has been achieved. In contrast, the terms 'facilitative', 'elaborated' and 'divergent' highlight quite a different approach with a different less defined outcome. Closer inspection of the research evidence seems to be conveyed in papers that synthesise evidence on feedback. These tend to be based on quantitative data that place greater emphasis on the effectiveness of the more focused approaches, simply for the reason that they more easily yield quantitative data connected with outcomes. When meta-analysis draws only on quantitative data, some of the more process-driven approaches that require more complex and less tangible understandings become more marginalised. Therefore, their influence and relevance may be no less important but they become less visible in data which is designed to be 'visible' (Hattie, 2009). The literature points to the importance of both types of approaches being important (e.g. Shute, 2008; Torrance and Pryor, 1998). However, what is also increasingly clear is that in real classroom contexts, drawing together both approaches is not straightforward. In a performance-driven educational climate, processes which seek particular tangible outcomes tend to favour more focused visible feedback approaches. Black (2015: 163) draws attention to the difficulties that teachers have in translating these more complex meanings and levels of evidence into their practice. More specific case studies further illustrate this point, such as chapter 7 in this book. Furthermore, studies by Hargreaves (2013), Murtagh (2014), and Torrance and Pryor (1998) give insight into the details of processes and interpretations, which make feedback more complex to both grasp and enact.

## Forms of feedback

Feedback may occur in many forms. Typically, it is considered as oral or written and is from a teacher to a pupil. Sadler (1989: 79) emphasises the point that the source of the feedback (whether teacher, pupil, computer) is less important than its validity. However, the issue of validity is not straightforward, and is revisited later in this chapter. There can be no assumption that the validity of feedback is seen in the same way by teachers and pupils. Sadler highlights the importance of how the feedback is framed. He particularly considers the importance of referencing feedback in terms of standards that are separate from other pupils or from pupils' previous attainments. That is, feedback that is neither norm referenced (in relation to others) or self-referenced (in relation to a pupil's past attainments). Essential for effective feedback, in Sadler's terms, is the skill of the teacher in providing task-related or standards-orientated feedback, which does not have normative interpretations (81). However, this must be undertaken using language that is already known and understood by the learner. This is because the learner's knowledge is incomplete and the teacher must be careful to frame feedback within pupils' understandings and terms of reference. Sadler also notes that teachers should not provide 'differential levels of feedback for learners', as matching feedback to different levels of performance, he considers, 'treats students inequitably' (82).

The emphasis here is on the preciseness of the feedback in relation to objective standards. This is echoed in other evidence about feedback effectiveness, which is related to specific outcomes. Particular discussion is offered about whether the feedback process should focus on goals or tasks. The distinction being that goals are slightly longer term and lie beyond an individual task. Understanding of how a task enables you to move towards a goal is considered to be an important motivator. Hence, feedback should help the learner understand and move towards the goal (Shute, 2008: 161). Tunstall and Gipps (1996), focusing on feedback to young children, identity a range of practices that involve task-related, goal-related, socialisation-focused and self-efficacy-related feedback in the form of rewarding and approving. They further illustrate the importance of feedback being related to a task or to learning, rather than directed to the self, as being more effective. Hattie and Timperley (2007) identify four different focuses for feedback: feedback on the task (FT); on the processes needed to complete the task (FP); on the process of self-regulation (FR); and on the individual person (self) involved (FS). The latter they identify as least effective. However, the research also recognises that a variety of forms of feedback is useful, but they have different roles and potential impact.

## Confusion and contradiction

What emerges from even a brief consideration of the literature is a confusing and even contradictory picture of feedback. Sadler's view (1989) is explored by way of illustration, partly because of the significance of his work within the feedback litera-ture, and also as an example of the tensions that permeate understandings beyond his particular work. Sadler advocates that feedback is best if specifically related to standards. Problems with the effectiveness of feedback, in Sadler's terms, are related to 'inadequately specified standards' when teachers default to an 'existentially determined baseline' (83) and thus include cohort or person-centred perspectives. Focus and precision on standards, which must be clearly defined and not related to the performance of others, is essential. However, Sadler also recognises that the language in which these standards are framed must be formed from language which children can understand. However, they should not have 'norm-relevant implications' (83). Sadler seems to be calling for a decontextualising of feedback which, in order to become most effective, needs to be more precise. However, recognition of the importance of the right language seems to raise an alternative, even conflicting perspective. Yet, although Sadler (1989: 83) acknowledges 'communication across the divide [*differences between teachers' and learners' knowledge and experience*] is an issue worthy of serious study', the omission of such study seems to render it as marginal to the more central issue of standards. Thus, specific consideration of individual pupil needs and the possibility of differentiating feedback according to learner needs, remains fairly marginal in contemporary debate.

Herein lies a significant problem with understanding feedback, which contributes to some of the confusing, competing and even contradictory research findings. Does effective feedback seek precision of delivery, and recognition of 'effectiveness' in terms of pre-defined standards being met? The literature makes it clear that such a tightly focused approach is inadequate. For feedback to be formative, the way it is understood and used by pupils must also be important. The literature does explore issues of impact and interpretation. However, this is largely contextualised as part of how feedback is used for an individual's self-regulatory process. This is briefly considered within the following section.

## Receiving feedback

A significant aspect of the literature on feedback relates to the response of recipients to feedback. Kluger and DeNisi (1996: 260) examine this in the context of how individuals might respond in order to shift the gap between their current attainment and their perception of what is being required – 'the standard gap'. They identify four possible responses, all of which reduce the 'standard gap' in their terms. First, they might increase their effort in order to move nearer towards the standards required. Second, they may just abandon the standard and not have it as part of their own learning gap. Third, they might change the standard so that it is more acceptable to their own framing of their learning gap. Fourth, they might reduce the feedback message (260). Each of these responses illustrate that the 'power of feedback' (to use Hattie and Timperley's phrase) does not lie solely with the technical precision of the content of feedback. Pupils' possible responses, according to Shute (2008: 157), are linked to their cognitive responses. Therefore, there is a cognitive reason related to why learners respond to feedback in the way that they do. The gap that the feedback might help define and explain may motivate the learner to respond in a way that reduces the gap. However, it may trigger greater uncertainty about learning, which could lead either to more effort or less effort being applied. The feedback may help to reduce the 'cognitive load' experienced by the learner. Here, the feedback may help to explain and scaffold the next learning steps, which will reduce the pressure from what might previously have seemed like a difficult step. Conversely, it may add to the 'cognitive load' in that the feedback sets out next steps, which a pupil feels to be unattainable.

Askew and Lodge (2000: 6) coined the term 'killer feedback' to describe feedback that blocks rather than facilitates learning. Thus, as Butler and Winne (1995: 248) highlight, external feedback 'may confirm, add to, or conflict with the learners' interpretations of the task and the path of learning'. Gamlem and Smith (2013) in exploring the response of 13–15 year-old pupils' perceptions of feedback, gave clear insight into their personal and emotional responses to feedback. Feedback valence (positive and negative), relationships as well as trust were highlighted as the main strands in their articulations of useful feedback. This contrasts with some of the more technical approaches that seek to understand feedback in terms of effectiveness.

What becomes important from analysing the available research is that not only does the type of feedback need to recognise that it might be required to address different aspects of learning, but it also must recognise the response (or likely response) from individual learners. The literature on feedback recognises that it can only be effective when it becomes part of a cognitive response, recognising that self-regulative processes become increasingly important as the learner takes on greater responsibility for creating and sustaining their own learning. Alongside this interplay of form and process is another crucial factor. This relates to a range of factors that shape the likelihood of self-regulatory process being developed. Literature on feedback affords particular significance to the role of learner disposition to the effectiveness of feedback. Black et al. (2006) highlight that 'intentional learners' gain most from feedback. Here the indication is that, no matter how the feedback is framed or focused, if the learner does not intend to learn then it will be of little use.

Further researchers reviewing feedback (Butler and Winne, 1995; Dann, 2016, Shute, 2008) have included Dweck's work on mindset. Dweck (2012) argues that the ways in which learners see and achieve their own goals will influence the way that they respond to feedback. She usefully summarises key strands from her research explaining the 'fixed mindset' and the 'growth mindset'. The fixed mindset is identified as an approach to learning in which learners tend to see their learning as limited to a particular set of abilities, which they already have. These may serve them well for the academic performances expected of them. However, when they are faced with learning that does not match these existing abilities, they are more reluctant to recognise the need to work at changing their learning. They are more likely to blame others or accept their failure (or reduced success). Those with a growth mindset are identified as having different views of their own learning. They recognise that their own efforts and persistence can make a difference to their learning futures. Feedback is likely to be regarded quite differently by these two types of learners. Those learners who recognise and actively engage in deliberately working on their learning strategies in order to keep increasing their learning capacity and capability are far more likely to seek out and use feedback than those who imagine that their learning skills are already fixed.

Of significance here is that the quality, design and structure of the feedback does not stand alone. Serious consideration must be given to the learners and their own approaches to learning. Much of the literature seems to indicate that variations in the impact of feedback may well be due to variation in pupil responses to learning.

What is perhaps less clear is the extent to which feedback may influence such intentions. Shute (2008) offers some insight here. In drawing on Hoska's work (1993) she suggests that feedback can modify learners' approaches to learning enabling them to be more responsive to feedback. As they begin to increase effort in response to feedback, they recognise it as part of their own cognitive support – this can subsequently shift their learning disposition. Although this research relates to computer-based feedback, it suggests that feedback can influence both learning outcomes and learning processes.

Feedback can therefore become information not just for changing learning outcomes, but also to help learners to think and plan their learning differently. As well as being part of their self-regulation, it becomes part of their metalearning and metacognition (Mylona, 2016). It potentially transforms not only their learning outcomes but also their ability to be a learner. It may thus help transformations of being a learner. But this transformational potential might not work positively for pupils. As Black and William (1998a: 18) point out, sometimes teachers' use of feedback tells 'the weaker pupils that they lack ability, so that they are de-motivated and lose confidence in their own capacity to learn'. Such understandings position feedback not only as a process used in assessment *for* learning (AfL), but also situates it as a tool which exemplifies assessment *as* learning (AaL) (Dann, 2014). Its role in shaping future learning, which might be both intended and unintended, perhaps offers some insight into why research on the impact of feedback yields such different evidence. As the discussion in this chapter has already highlighted, conceptualisation of feedback is varied. However, underpinning these conceptualisations are particular notions of 'validity' (a liberal interpretation), which are briefly examined next in order to both understand the problems and possibilities for understanding feedback.

## Considering 'validity'

Sadler (1989) identified that issues of validity in feedback are more important than the source of feedback. However, notions of validity are contested in education, and merit some attention here in order to understand their relevance for feedback. Barker (2013: 4) illustrates that it is a concept 'at war with itself'. This is partly because, within education, it has traditionally been used within a testing context. Typically, it has been framed through the Standards for Educational and Psychological Testing. These are a product of the American Educational Research Association, the American Psychological Association (APA), and the National Council on Measurement in Education (NCME). The focus is primarily on validity related to standardised tests. With this focus, validity is typically identified in relation to four key facets (the first of which is less likely to be a feature of all tests). First, predictive validity, which relates to the extent to which a test can predict future performance. Second, concurrent validity, which focuses on the extent to which one test will yield similar results to another test designed for the same purpose and focus. Third, content validity, which is related to whether a test adequately measures the content or domain at which it is aimed. Finally, construct validity, which relates to content validity but looks more specifically at whether the test captures the underlying skills (constructs) which reflect the domain to be tested.

Debate for several decades about validity has extended from trying to unify the concept (Messick, 1989) to 'deconstructing' it (Newton and Shaw, 2014). Further-more, debate has ranged from those who promote validity in its traditionalist sense to those who adopt a more liberal stance. Newton and Shaw (2016), suggest that a traditional conservative or even 'ultra' conservative perceptive focuses on mea-surement quality, and is mainly located in its endeavour to ensure that a test mea-sures what it is intended to measure. At the more liberal end of the debate is the notion that the consequences of testing (and interpretations of testing), whether intended or unintended, are also part of validity. This extends the discussion beyond the technical measurement factor of the test to its application, context and the interpretation which it uses. As Messick (1989: 19) first noted, 'social values cannot be ignored in consideration of validity'. Yet, he also clearly notes (Messick, 1989) that his consideration of 'consequential validity' is not intended to apportion blame to test constructors (or text users) and focus on test misuse, but to raise the issue that the consequences of test structure, content and purpose all need to be considered.

The consideration of validity so far, and in much of the literature, is focused specifically on standardised testing situations. A considerable part of the debate centres on the scientific exactitude with which a test can control conditions, measure specified content or constructs, and be interpreted in a precise way. The contra-dictions and differences in conceptualisation of validity are extensively linked to the extent to which human and social factors, which are less easy to fix and measure, are included in the discussion. Consideration of validity issues in this chapter are linked to their importance in a broader context within formative assessment. Thus they shift the debate away from testing and bring to the fore issues related to both teaching and learning. In the eyes of traditionalists, validity issues might seem irre-levant to formative assessment processes. Yet, as Sadler indicates, the importance of assessment being clearly focused on what it is intended to measure, its particular intended use, its interpretation, and its consequences are all important. Stobart (2006: 134) echoes the importance of validity being a significant issue for formative assessment and claims that it is 'essentially about fitness for purpose'. Crooks et al. (1996) identify that validity may be weakened at many points and these will change according to the type of assessment and its purpose. They offer an example about feedback suggesting that validity of feedback is threatened if 'it does not help and motivate students to improve their performance' (281). Hargreaves (2007: 185) further points to the importance of recognising that 'assessment for learning with high validity *actually* promotes learning'.

Validity issues are clearly important for developing understanding and use of feedback. A key dimension of feedback, to which notions of validity have reso-nance, is the extent to which feedback is focused on the learning that needs to be modified. Furthermore, the ways in which the feedback is conveyed can be seen as valid in terms of the likely response from learners in altering their learning. Both construct and content validity are therefore important. Consequential validity is essential, as feedback within formative assessment is all about consequences – future learning.

The fundamental arguments underpinning debate about issues of validity mirror some of the contradictions inherent in discussions about feedback. When tightly focused, with pre-constructed frameworks, specific goals, content and structural issues, feedback research makes claims about its effectiveness. Similarly, in standardised testing, when linked specifically to content and structure, validity claims are stronger. In both cases, as soon as the focus shifts to consideration of individual and social issues, to consequences, impact and interpretation, claims about effectiveness become far harder to evidence. Such considerations lie at the heart of many discords in education. The importance of validity in feedback is clearly important. However, when other factors are considered, each has its own validity claims (Habermas, 1984).

There can be no assumption that validity is seen in the same way by teachers and pupils. Chapters 7 and 8 in this book return to explore these differences in more detail. Thus, understanding and applying notions of validity for feedback call for the following questions to be asked:

• Does the feedback reflect its intended focus?
• Do all participants have a shared focus?
• To whom and for what purposes is the feedback valid?
• Is the learning climate conducive for feedback to have an impact?
• Who decides the validity of the impact and over what period of time?

Such considerations lead to a far more complex picture than might be evident in some of the research strands offered in the research literature. This is particularly the case in research that seeks to identify 'what works' in ways that are considered 'valid' against specific notions of curriculum content for particular outcomes.

## Limits to our understanding of feedback.

The purpose of this chapter was to set out what we know about feedback. What is clear is that feedback has a powerful impact. However, this impact may be positive or negative. There are some suggestions that help to point us in the direction of what might be more positive. Nevertheless, it is clear from the research that there is little agreement leading us to a straightforward model or recipe for 'effective' feedback. What can be distilled is that when feedback is tightly focused and precise it might help learners who are 'intentional learners' or whose own goals and aspirations are well aligned to the feedback offered. The research also points to the possibility of feedback helping less able learners too. Black and Wiliam (1998c) say 'improved formative assessment helps low achievers more than other students' (3) However, each learner will receive and interpret feedback in his/her own way, which may or may not match the intentions of those who offered the feedback. This potentially locates feedback as one dimension of each learner's learning environment. It sets feedback as a form of communication within a space. A space that is both physical, a space that is cognitive (between learning now and learning next) and a space that is about values as much as knowledge. It positions feedback as part of the actions of pupils as well as part of the actions of teachers. It frames feedback as a communicative tool in which the message does not flow simply in one direction. It requires greater understanding and more nuanced consideration from both teachers and pupils, and their interaction through feedback processes. The research indicates the necessity of such an approach, yet also declares that feedback tends to be highly controlled by teachers:

> The power dynamic between those who give feedback and those who are on the receiving end has not shifted very far … because the agenda is not decided by the person who 'receives' the feedback, it may not be useful to them, or they may not know how to make use of it.
>
> *(Askew and Lodge, 2000: 10)*

Even when more interactive approaches to feedback are introduced, they tend to be constrained. Leganger-Krogstad (2014) indicates that dialogic approaches often become 'forced dialogue', which is mainly linked to teachers' priorities. This echoes Lefstein's (2010) claims that tensions between rules and relationships often constrain the way in which more interactive approaches might be developed within school systems. Yet, despite these difficulties it is clear that failure to understand the pupil in the context of feedback will be of little help. Furthermore, if feedback is to be understood as part of formative assessment (Assessment for Learning) it relates to the future and to future actions. It is a bridge between the past, present and future and spans a cognitive space between now and next. It is also part of an interactive encounter with learning. All of these factors, and particularly their interconnection, seem inadequately considered in the literature, and in the way feedback is conceptualised and enacted. It is the intention that this book will help to re-examine and synthesise a different way of making sense of feedback which draws together some of the literature, and positions feedback into different understandings of pupil and teachers. It specially locates it as relational communicative action which is part of both AfL and AaL.

**PART II**

# Conceptualising the learning gap

# 4

# CONCEPTUALISING THE LEARNING GAP

## A deterministic approach

### Chapter overview

This chapter is one of three that will look more closely at the notion of the 'learning gap'. Discussion about feedback is located within the notion of a learning gap, and how feedback alters the gap. Who defines and controls the learning gap, and for what or whose purposes is unclear. Different constructions of a pupil's learning gap linked to feedback have received little examination within national and international debates. What has received more attention is the 'gap' between the educational performances of different categories of pupils within countries, as well as the 'gap' between the performances of pupil cohorts between countries measured through international test comparisons. The key focus in this chapter relates to exploring how and why what children learn in school is identified and regulated both nationally and internationally. Particular considerations are explored in terms of how what children need to know, and are expected to know, are externally determined. This creates a particular version of their learning gap, which is both national and internationally constructed. I have framed this way of seeking the learning gap as a 'deterministic approach'. Furthermore, the gap that is created between learning now and learning next, becomes a 'zone of expectation'.

Conceptualising the learning gap in this way also links to how it has a particular framing on teaching and learning, and the form and function of the feedback mechanisms used to interconnect them. It highlights particular considerations for examining how feedback to pupils about their learning becomes coded in specific ways, constructing and shaping the learning gap for children in pre-determined ways. The framing of pupil performances in national and international high-stakes systems prioritises pupils as a collective. In Au's terms (2011: 37) they 'objectify students by reducing them into decontextualized numerical objectives for comparison', rather than as individuals. Yet, what becomes significant, and in need of further exploration, is the way in which these approaches can be understood in the real spaces in which teaching and learning happen. In this chapter, two key themes are examined initially in order to understand the policy context both internationally and nationally against which a better understanding of a deterministic approach to understanding the learning gap can be outlined. First, the rise of global educational policy governance will be examined. Second, attention is directed to the purpose of high-stakes testing. Following these two sections, the chapter offers new insights into how feedback is understood and constructed from such a perspective.

## The impact of global educational policy governance

Ozga (2009: 150) highlighted the change in policy meta-narrative from 'government to governance' in explaining the considerable shift in how education, and particularly knowledge (meaning 'learning'), is understood and regulated. The significant shift relates to new understandings of knowledge, and knowledge production, as economies become 'Knowledge Economies'. As Ozga explains (2008: 265), this concerns world-leading economies positioning knowledge as essential to their economic productivity and growth. What matters in this meta-narrative is that knowledge is seen as a global commodity. If appropriately harnessed, it will lead to increased economic performance. Ozga (2008) argues that knowledge becomes a key output but is also inherent in legitimising and supporting the political process through claiming that certain types of knowledge will 'scientifically' lead to more effective outcomes. Thus, knowledge becomes central as both a product and a process. To these ends standardised testing becomes a technical tool for measuring outcomes and a calculative rationality promoted through the 'apparently neutral and objective language of science' (Ozga, 2008: 265), which is used to create a policy narrative around what is desirable, excellent and 'what works'.

With this new focus on 'Knowledge Economies', international competitiveness on the global economic stage is increasingly played out in the way knowledge outcomes are measured. Education therefore moves centre stage, and standardised testing becomes 'the chief instrument of educational governance' (Tröhler, 2010: 6). Thus, the importance of education becomes ever more important as global economies require a skilled and adaptable workforce in order to respond to, as well as be pioneering in, a changing and uncertain world. As countries refine and reshape their education systems in order to develop the education of their pupils, significant attention is increasingly given to analysing and comparing 'big data' from international standardised testing (Crossley, 2014). Accordingly, policy watching and policy borrowing from countries deemed successful becomes more prevalent.

Finding evidence for what is considered 'successful', therefore, becomes prized knowledge in this global hunt for the best performing education system. It seems that the key answers to the questions of who does best in education is to be found through the scores published from international testing data. This quantified approach to understanding learning (knowledge) illustrates the authoritative role that numbers (test data) are given in representing educational realities. Even though such representations are challenged within educational research (Goldstein and Moss, 2014), interpretation continues in order to sustain, and in Ozga's terms (2008), 'fabricate' notions of quality and achievement in educational policy and progress.

Most notable in this international arena for measuring the quality of international educational performance in our knowledge economies is PISA data (Programme for International Student Assessment). Promoted through the OECD (Office for Economic Co-operation and Development), this event for 15-year-olds, held every three years, offers outcomes-based evidence which is often used by governments as a basis for their educational policy review and development. The type of competence assessed through PISA focuses on real-life challenges rather than content mastery. In 2012, 34 OECD member countries engaged in this process along with 31 other countries. The data from PISA in 2015 reveals 72 participating countries. In 2012, PISA focused on mathematics, with science and reading having less prominence. Each three-year cycle focuses on one of the three subject areas. The UK was 26th for mathematics, 21st in science and 23rd in reading, with all of its score near the OECD average. All three scores illustrated fairly stable results over the last decade (Wheater et al., 2014). From the 2015 data (the focus subject being science) the UK dropped to 27th for mathematics, rose to 15th in science, although its point score dropped, and rose to 22nd in reading. Even with some small rises in positioning, the scores were still near to the OECD average. England performed better in relation to the other countries of the UK within this statistic in all areas in 2015. What is revealing is how this data becomes drawn into national policy developments for participating countries. It does so in a way that overrides and steers national levels of educational policy making. Lingard (2010: 136) examines such phenomena indicting that national levels of policy are overlaid by data from international policy instruments. He identifies this shift as a 'principle of global policy convergence'.

In England, such a policy shift is clearly evident. The government White Paper (2016) *Educational Excellence Everywhere* indicated that its static position on PISA compared to other countries was unacceptable. 'Other education systems from Shanghai to Singapore to Poland and Germany – are improving faster than we are' (para 1.7, p. 6). Furthermore, PISA data reveals that across the whole of the UK poor children are worse off at every stage. 'We have a long tail of low attainment – 17% of UK students fail to reach "modern functional literacy" compared with just 11% in Canada' (para 1.8, p. 6). This information is even more compounded by a recognition that England's own internal qualifications processes have reported steady increases in pupil achievements at the age of 16, which are not evidenced in international performance data comparisons. Thus, the international policy data is overlaid and reflected in the White Paper through its conclusion that 'for too long, qualifications in this country suffered from grade inflation – from 2000–2012, GCSE grades rose steeply, but assessments benchmarked internationally showed no corresponding rise in mathematics' (para 6.61, p. 91). This prompts a new way of looking at national assessment and markers of quality, which are directly steered by this principle of global policy convergence.

It is clear from PISA data that the type of learning being tested concerns the application of knowledge to real-life situations and that pupils are given one attempt to sit each subject. The increase in grades for the GCSE qualifications (General Certificate in Secondary Education) may be related to the different type of knowledge sought as well as being related to the fact that until 2015 pupils could sit and resit the many parts of the GCSE papers until (hopefully) they increased their scores. Little discussion is centred on these different foci, and the differences in learning (knowledge) being sought through each. Radical reform of national qualifications in England (both GCSE and Advanced (A) level) specially seeks to address this.

Global policy convergence, regulated and justified through international (independent) standardised tests, serving the purpose of providing measurable data, and offering a justification for testing as a means of driving up standards, frames human capital and economic competitiveness in particular ways. Of particular interest in this chapter is the way human capital is understood, shaped and promoted. Education, within this global policy arena, conceptualises children and their learning in particular (unstated) ways. Although this will be discussed more fully in the final section of this chapter, Au (2011: 26) offers a view that encapsulates the argument that is being built. He claims, 'Standardized tests themselves, through the inter-related processes of decontextualization, objectification and commodification, fundamentally provide the foundational basis for education to be framed as a form of factory production.' How such a perspective might be translated in the classroom is important to examine. Therefore, it is to the context of the classroom that attention is now turned to see how the ever increasing status of high stakes testing plays out. More particularly, attention is focused on the significance of international and national policy on the realities of teaching and learning in schools.

## High-stakes national testing in England

To add to the discussion outlined above, further arguments suggest that teaching and learning within these shifting converging global policy contexts are significantly related to the requirements of tests and examinations. As the accountability systems for school success are measured in terms of test outcomes, pupil achievements in tests matter more. At all levels, pupils' achievements in tests are high stakes. Accordingly, 'teachers are teaching to the test with increasing regularity, consistency and intensity' (Au, 2011: 30).

In England, from age 6 they are tested in their phonics abilities through a phonics screening test. At age 7, they are tested in spelling, punctuation and grammar tests. Computerised times tables tests are planned for introduction at age 11 and new 'attainment 8' measures for GCSE are in place at age 16. The need to ensure that pupils meet 'floor standards' (minimum standards) and 'expected levels' becomes critical in seeking to ensure that attainment is considered acceptable in standards-based testing frameworks. The focus of these tests mirrors those prioritised internationally, yet within the national system in England they provide essential data for the judgements made on individual schools by the regulatory inspecting body (Ofsted – Office for Standards in Education). The evidence points to data provided from these tests dominating the outcomes of inspections, and thus determining and framing school 'success'.

The emphasis on evidence-based quantifiable test-driven systems is firmly linked to a national education policy agenda associating rigorous assessments with raising standards. What became more evident was the widening gap between the achievements of the poorest pupils (from families identified as being of low social economic status (SES)) and other children. This led to a new focus centred in ensuring that all children were achieving. The Secretary of State for Education, Nicky Morgan, in the 2016 White Paper (*Educational Excellence Everywhere*) declared that the government 'are unapologetically ambitious for every child, no matter what their background, prior attainment or needs' (para 6.1, p. 88). Such a view had developed from the shift in the focus of attention in the Ofsted framework to examine school performance data related to the gap between pupils classified as having 'free school meals' (fsm) and others. If there were a significant gap in both progress and achievement between those pupils categorised as having 'fsm' and other children in school performance data, schools were considered to be underperforming. Thus, the new 'game' for schools was not just to get as many children to the expected level as possible but to demonstrate that the progress and attainment of its children from lower social economic status matched the attainment of other children. Extra funding was allocated to each pupil in the lower economic grouping to help fund the extra support that they might need (Pupil Premium funds).

Pratt (2016) gives an interesting insight into how such high-stakes assessment is played out in primary schools through discussion with teachers. His research, drawing on Bourdieu's work, highlights significant game playing by teachers in ensuring that their pupils achieve at the required level. He also points to the particular relationship teachers have with students who fall below the required expected scores. Not only do these children pose a problem for the school in terms of published school data but also for the teacher in terms of his/her personal performance management. Thus, 'pupils' outcomes are used to differentiate them in terms of their value in this process' (14). Pratt indicates here that pupils become valued in different ways according to the extent to which they serve the requirements of both the school and the teacher, within the neoliberal agenda.

This shift in emphasis from raising standards to raising standards for all so that all are expected to achieve the same standard, has had a significant influence in schools. The shift in emphasis on outcomes was also accompanied by a change in the national structure of determining national achievement expectations. Prior to this White Paper (2016), the government had removed a long-established structure to the way in which the National Curriculum was assessed. It introduced a new system … 'assessment without levels' (DfE, 2015).

The National Curriculum in England, first established in 1988, was structured around an assessment system that identified what children should know, through a series of levels. Notionally, children would increase one level about every two years. National tests and reporting would use these levels to identify the percentage of pupils achieving the expected levels at the end of Key Stage 1 (age 7) and Key Stage 2 (age 11). Their design originated through the Task Group on Assessment and Testing (DfES, 1988). The national assessment system was heralded as achieving the impossible. It claimed to offer a revolutionary solution of balancing the differing purposes of formative, summative, diagnostic and evaluative assessment (para. 23). However, over two decades later, National Curriculum levels were deemed unfit for purpose. What became clear was that schools were being measured on the percentage of pupils gaining expected National Curriculum levels and their achievements benchmarked against national averages. Failure to achieve the national average resulted in schools being deemed as failing. What resulted was that pupils who were at the borderline or just sitting under the threshold of the expected level were the focus for greater teaching attention, as increasing their results into the expected level could alter the outcome for the school. Those pupils who were well below the threshold, with little chance of achieving it, as well as those who might be well above seemed to matter less. As in the US, the testing system, designed to serve pupils, parents and communities to drive up standards, was quickly distorted into game playing to gain the best results for an outcomes measure centred mainly on getting as many pupils as possible past a determined threshold level. As the Commission on Assessment without Levels state in their final report (DfE, 2015), the whole assessment system related to levels was used by 'some teachers simply to track pupils towards target levels. The drive for progress across levels also led teachers to focus their attention disproportionately on pupils just below level boundaries' (13).

## High-stakes national testing in the United States of America

Certainly, these problems were not unique to the UK. The high-stakes nature of tests in both the UK and USA has caused a response from their respective political systems. Since George W. Bush's presidency, the No Child Left Behind (NCLB) Act in 2001 was introduced. At its start every child would be tested, by law, in reading and mathematics at three stages during their schooling. The number of tests required under NCLB increased up to 17 per child in the USA. Ravitch (2010) commented that NCLB signalled a new type of school reform, characterised by 'accountability, high-stakes testing, data-driven decision-making, choice, charter schools, privatisation, deregulation, meritpay and competition between schools. Whatever could not be measured did not count' (217).

Within Barak Obama's presidency further incentives were given for increased testing. This followed the economic crisis that had effectively lowered local revenues funding education. To help ensure that school standards were supported, the Obama administration funded millions of dollars to fund 'Race to the Top' (launched in 2012). By the end of the academic year 2014/15 the average pupil was taking 112 mandatory tests from pre-kindergarten to the end of high school (according to the Council of the Great City Schools, 2015). As Hursh (2013: 575) identifies, the significance of high-stakes testing is part of a neoliberal agenda which seeks to increase school privatisation as a response to standards not sufficiently rising (575). Policies become more centralised and directly regulated by test outcomes, which although developed and administered at state and federal levels, form a national policy drive.

Particular emphasis was placed on ensuring that low-income students were adequately progressing. If test results did not show progress over five consecutive years then whole school administrations would be changed. In response to such requirements, schools added their own tests in an attempt to ensure pupils were on track. The pressure mounted for teaching tactics that would show the required results. Tanner (2013), in exploring the impact of the 'Race to the Top' policy, draws attention to the narrowing of the curriculum (a convergent curriculum). He questions the notion of high-stakes testing in terms of the type of knowledge and engagement that the multiple-choice-framed testing structure promotes. Given that teaching becomes more focused on the tests, he puzzles over why 'technocrats who created the multiple-choice test should seek to re-create the human mind in the multiple-choice image' (6).

With a change in curriculum following the introduction of the US Common Core, new Common Core tests were introduced in early 2015. However, across many states the implementation of the tests proved disastrous as the computer-based systems repeatedly crashed, leaving children staring at blank screens part way through their tests. With parents increasingly unhappy about the pressure of tests, and a new system of tests that could not be effectively administered, US President Obama suddenly stated in October 2015:

> When I look back on the great teachers that shaped my life, what I remember isn't the way they prepared me to take standardised tests ... I've heard from teachers who feel so much pressure to teach to a test that it takes the joy out of teaching and learning, both for them and for the students. I want to fix that.
>
> (Obama, 2015b)

With the replacement of NCLB with the 'Every Child Succeeds' Act, testing still remained. However, the US Department of Education states that no more than two per cent of class time should be on assessment testing. Furthermore, provision for auditing preparation for testing so that overtesting can be identified has been introduced. In a statement in October 2015 it stated:

> In too many schools, there is unnecessary testing and not enough clarity of purpose applied to the task of assessing students, consuming too much instructional time and creating undue stress for educators and students. The Administration bears some of the responsibility for this, and we are committed to being part of the solution.
>
> (US Department of Education 2015)

This reveals the realisation that the testing system was indeed shaping teaching and learning in particular ways, which were firstly not intended, and secondly not desirable.

## Inequalities and testing outcomes

Particular insight into further examining the effect of high-stakes testing has been highlighted by Dorling (2015). Countries in which there is a greater gap between rich and poor within their economies seem to have a different relationship between education, outcomes and examinations in the 16–25 age bracket from countries that display less societal inequalities. Dorling suggests that the countries with wide differences between rich and poor, such as the US and UK, fail to foster long-lasting learning when pupils finish their exams at age 16. So although their learning in the PISA tests may be seen as average, the results in PIAAC (Program for the International Assessment of Adult Competencies) for 16–24-year-olds reveal a different picture. When the results at age 15 are compared with those of the 15–24 age bracket, there is an increasingly strong correlation between countries with high inequalities and a larger gap between the two scores. Dorling suggests that in these countries with high inequalities the pay gap in different sectors of the market is large. Gaining the best qualifications thus matters more. Schools and parents are keen for threshold levels to be met at age 16 in terms of gaining high exam grades. Dorling suggests that because the stakes are high for schools and for families, methods are used that focus on optimum exam success. Thus, short-term teaching to the test methods seem to take priority, often resulting in the information being quickly forgotten. Those countries nearer the top of both PISA and PIAAC have traditionally had much smaller levels of inequality. As Dorling suggests, the possible link cannot be ignored. What he adds to the discussion is that not only are the results for the UK on PISA mediocre, but post 16 these mediocre scores diminish more rapidly than in other countries with less of a gap between rich and poor.

## Teaching and learning within high-stakes assessment systems

The preceding discussion drawn from both US and UK examples illustrates how high-stakes testing drives schools to game play in order to gain the best outcomes within performance orientated systems. As governments seek to use these outcome measures, they also seek to provide solutions for schools to enable them to reach the required standards. Importing practices from the countries at the top of the PISA league tables seems to feature highly in these policy borrowing activities, notably from the countries of the Far East. The top five performing jurisdictions in mathematics in 2012 were Shanghai, Singapore, Hong Kong, Taiwan and South Korea. The White Paper (DfE, 2016), in recognising and responding to England's static position in PISA reports that 35 maths hubs have been established that have sent teachers to Shanghai and have also trialled English adapted maths textbooks for primary schools from Singapore (para 6.13). Furthermore, a mastery approach is being promoted 'to ensure that no pupil's understanding is left to chance, and each step in a lesson is deliberate, purposeful and precise' (para 6.13, p. 91).

Whether such initiatives will gain the desired results remain questionable. Testing mastery of knowledge is clearly stated by PISA as *not* being the focus of its tests. 'Rather than examine mastery of specific school curricula, PISA looks at students' ability to apply knowledge and skills in key subject areas and to analyse, reason and communicate effectively as they examine, interpret and solve problems' (OECD, http://www.oecd.org/pisa/aboutpisa/pisafaq.htm). Thus, there seems to be some lack of understanding, or at least lack of synergy, between the form and purpose of international testing measures (focused on applied knowledge) and national ones. Clearly, in the UK, with the removal of national levels and guidance offered to help schools determine pupils' expected achievements, there is a shift to 'mastery' learning. Even though this is not the focus of PISA, there may be some sense in which such an approach may help to secure knowledge better, allowing future applications of learning to be made more successfully.

> The new national curriculum is premised on this kind of understanding of mastery, as something which every child can aspire to and every teacher should promote. It is about deep, secure learning for all, with extension of able students (more things on the same topic) rather than acceleration (rapidly moving on to new content). Levels were not consistent with this approach because they encouraged undue pace and progression onto more difficult work while pupils still had gaps in their knowledge or understanding. In developing new approaches to assessment, schools have the opportunity to make 'mastery for all' a genuine goal.
> *(DfE, 2015: 17)*

Furthermore, the national textbook approach is a feature across many successful countries, including Japan and Finland. It has not been a pervading feature of UK education up until 2017, although its inclusion within the White Paper (DfE, 2016) is perhaps a strong indicator that this may change. Understanding what it is we are measuring, and how it is best measured, seems somewhat confused. In recognising global policy convergence combined with policy borrowing to serve outcome-orientated performance-driven national and global education systems, there is significant incongruence in how national and international systems synchronise understanding of what standards in education look like and mean. This leads to considerable problems for schools in trying to determine how best to enable the outcomes that assessments require. If PISA requires 'applied learning' and national systems seek 'mastery learning', are there conflicts, confusions and tensions that form barriers rather than a bridge to developing learning?

## National and international framing of the learning gap

The way in which PISA seems to fuel discussion of talk about 'gaps' (Hardy, 2015: 469) gives insight into the way in which learning and the gap between what is known and what is not known is articulated. Drawn from PISA data, 'gaps' are framed in terms of collective national attainment standardised test results compared globally (among OECD member countries), as well as the relative attainments of sub groups, such as between boys and girls, and those educated in private compared to public schools. This transnational framing is based on averages, and the media quickly present global hierarchies of assumed knowledge attainment. This understanding of a learning gap is highly significant for individual countries. In the UK the data is interpreted to clearly identify that our national learning gap is too large. UK children are thus identified in English education policy as 'deficient' in terms of our national learning achievements in relation to other countries that are above us on the PISA league table. This is even though England is above the OECD average. Secondly, by implication within government policy, it renders our education system as deficient as it fails to deliver outcomes that match other countries. It overrides any successes that may be identified within our own education system, which might show increasing levels of achievement and/or higher national averages. It identifies a national learning gap, framed by the testing outcomes of PISA, which is measured only through a sample of 15-year-old children's results, who are regarded collectively as a single cohort.

The learning gap in this context is constructed in generalised terms using processes that measure total and average scores from a sample, and then compares these scores. In all participating countries in which OECD carries out PISA, a random sample of schools is selected and within these schools a randomly selected sample of pupils is chosen. Such an approach is designed to statistically accommodate for any disadvantages of any particular grouping. It is also designed to offer a stable and valid data set. As Meyer and Benavot (2013) indicate, this approach certainly dominates the discourse in global discussions of standards in education. As this chapter has illustrated, this international approach, together with national testing frameworks, have come to define teaching and learning in recent years and what the outcomes of education should look like. Such approaches to measuring the outcomes of education have become the catalyst for changes to contemporary national policy. Increasingly, these policies seek to structure and stage education in particular 'scientifically proven' ways. As Tanner (2013) observes, teaching and learning become more mechanised through a belief that particular scientifically evidenced approaches will enhance grade outcomes.

Such Taylorised practices were becoming more evident in the US (and the UK). More specially in the UK, there are a growing number of randomised control trial studies, funded through the government's Education Endowment Fund, particularly concerned with seeking to provide the 'best' approach for the most vulnerable pupils. The *Education Excellence Everywhere* White Paper (2016) further supports this approach with its stated intention to promote a 'what works' approach through a designated What Works Centre for Education (para 2.63) as well as seeking to ensure that research is accessible and relevant to schools.

## System-level feedback for learning in the global classroom

What is clear from the analysis and discussion offered in this chapter is that teaching and learning are structured in particular predetermined ways. Learning is heavily centred on that which is tested. This becomes increasingly structured in ways that lend themselves to measurement. The learning gap for each child becomes a 'zone of expectation' that is externally defined and measured. In England the emphasis on decoding isolated words (real words and nonsense words) based on phonics denotes success in year 1 (children age 6). New spelling, grammar and punctuation tests (SPaG) require a highly technical approach to grammar. These determine success in year 2 (age 7), and year 6 (aged 11). Such focused grammatical questions stumped the Secretary of State for Schools (Nick Gibb) who was unable to answer correctly, even though he admitted that he was familiar with the question. He was asked the following question in a live Radio 4 'News at One' programme: In the sentence 'I went to the cinema after I'd eaten my dinner', is the word 'after' a sub-ordinating conjunction or a preposition? This was from a test aimed at 11-year-olds. Unfortunately, he gave the answer 'preposition', which is incorrect (BBC3, May 2016). Nevertheless, he continued his insistence that such tests were important.

It illustrates that neither the content of the tests nor the testing procedures used are negotiable. The feedback from the government in England is that such tests are essential for driving up standards and becoming more internationally competitive, and are part of the government's response to the fact that even after 25 years of a national curriculum with national testing, '1 in 3 children left primary school unable to read, write and add up properly; where the number of young people studying core subjects had halved in 13 years' (DfE, 2016: 3). The feedback from the government is clear, that learning is not good enough, and without external structured and focused testing in particular core areas of education, will not improve.

In addition to this feedback, it is also clear that any gains in improvement that the English education system might report, such as the increased national average of 16-year-old pupils gaining expected levels in national examinations and more schools being judged by Ofsted as 'good' or 'outstanding', there is insufficient progress in internal PISA scores. 'Our standards have remained static, at best, whilst other countries have moved ahead' (DfE, 2016: 3). This, combined with the decision to raise the requirements for 11-years-olds, yielded a marked decline in the percentage of pupils gaining the nationally expected results from over 80 per cent to 53 per cent (in 2016).

Of primary importance, therefore, in UK education policy making is the nation's performance and position revealed through the results of international tests. As a consequence, the gap between the nation's achievements and those of other countries, whose higher achievements positioned them above, is considered too great. This in turn defines the learning gap between the knowledge of all the children in our nation as being below what is required to increase our global position. The learning gap is shaped by the gap between our test results and the results of children in more highly achieving countries. This reality cannot be ignored. As this chapter has illustrated, the framing of a nation's learning gap is highly significant in the global educational arena. As this chapter has sought to outline, the impact of this overarching assessment-driven global achievement framework permeates and influences teaching and learning through the policy changes that result. When we look at the definition of feedback (chapter 3), it is clear that feedback is about altering a gap between where you are and where you want to be. Feedback must therefore contain information that is sufficiently specific for it to be used to alter the gap. Certainly, within the context of this chapter, national policy seeks to shift education practices in order to achieve a closing of this global performance gap. Thus the information from the global assessments certainly frames a learning gap for each country (in relation to other countries), but it does not offer information on how to close the gap. To some extent the policies that nations subsequently develop as they strategise to move up the PISA rankings (or other international testing scales) become a form of specific feedback for the school system, designed to close this national learning gap.

The extent to which it achieves this is not an issue for further discussion in this chapter. What is of interest, however, is how national educational policy provides a form of feedback designed to bring about changes to national achievement levels. Its nature and purpose are constructed in ways that will refocus the outcomes of schooling, and thus are designed to improve performance in these tests. Given that these tests are about national cohorts based on standardised random samples of 15-year-olds, the basis of the feedback and the understanding of the outcomes of learning are pitched at a mass population level, at a system level, and are very different from the feedback that much of this book is about. Nevertheless, the considerations outlined in this chapter provide an important overlay. They provide the context in which classroom-based formative assessment, teaching and learning operate.

The purpose in offering this chapter is far from a diversion from feedback within formative assessment. It seeks to understand a particular narrative of feedback for learning through the policies which seek to shape the nation's learning outcomes and attainment. Every school and every pupil is located within this national framing of the learning gap. This is a pre-defined space with its outer limits constructed by the global testing measures used by the OECD. Within this space is a further layer of national testing and exposing of standards. Individual pupils are anonymised and seen as a collective in terms of their results. There is little doubt that this reality will not diminish in the near future. However, there are signs that alongside this performance agenda greater recognition needs to be given to the individual pupils and to reducing the extent to which test-focused practices prevail in classrooms.

Consideration of how national and global context shape the 'learning gap' in particular ways reveals that the priorities nationally and internationally quickly dominate classroom practices. Lingard (2010) pointed out his view on 'global policy convergence', in which global policies become overlaid on national and local levels, and differences between countries begin to reduce. Similarly, practices in classrooms become increasingly shaped by these policies, and also begin to converge. Classrooms begin to seek technical measures and approaches that will give them greatest gains. Teaching practice thus becomes more framed by these predetermined outcomes. This gives context and background for why practices such as feedback tend to reflect this deterministic agenda, even though they are intended to be a process used between teachers and pupils in classrooms (chapter 7 develops this in context).

## Challenges to the deterministic approach

Three final examples are offered, illustrating how this deterministic approach is being challenged and reshaped. Firstly, at a national level, a series of episodes in England in April and May 2016 linked to the administering of standard tests gave further 'feedback' about the content and processes of the testing approach. It mirrored similar events and controversies experienced in the US. On 3 May, the same day as Nick Gibb (Minister of State in the Department for Education) revealed his own lack of essential standard knowledge of grammar, parents across the country staged the first attempt to remove their children from classrooms in protest against the tests. (In total, the numbers were not large – about 2,000.) Feedback to the government was clear through the campaign 'Let our kids be kids', which organised the protest and had gained over 45,000 signatures on a petition against the level of testing in the English education system (*Telegraph* 3/5/2016).

Further feedback was received from the teaching unions following several blunders resulting in tests being leaked. In April 2016 one of the Key Stage 1 live tests was mistakenly released prior to it being taken. Furthermore, on 10 May a rogue marker put a Key Stage 2 test paper online the day it was due to be taken. Feedback from the general secretary of the largest teaching union, Christine Blower, stated 'the whole of primary assessment in 2016 has been nothing but chaos and confusion'. Similar statements followed from the other teaching unions (Bullard, 2016: 8–9).

Teachers and head teachers offered their feedback. On 10 May the national press reported that children were distressed and many in tears as the reading test for 11-year-olds was the hardest it had ever been. Bullard, writing in the *Times Educational Supplement*, commented:

> We have had a fairly relaxed approach to SATS ... But this year we have felt compelled to teach more to the tests than ever before ... My staff and children could not have worked any harder and I feel sad for my year 6 children in particular.
>
> *(Bullard, 2016: 9)*

The *Times Educational Supplement* (13/5/2016) reported that 89 per cent of teachers want SATs abolished.

The second example is at a school level and has gained significant national attention. As the national tests in England approached in 2016, Jennie King, head teacher at Willesborough School in Kent, sent a letter to her year 6 pupils, which included these words:

> The SATS tests do not assess all of what makes each of you special and unique ... The levels that you get from these tests will tell you something but they will not tell you everything. There are many ways of being smart ... So while you are preparing for the tests and in the midst of it all, remember that there is no way to 'test' all of the amazing and awesome things that make you YOU.

This was not the first letter of this kind to have been reported in either the UK or US. It illustrated a particular type of approach seeking to value pupils in a testing system that is seen to dehumanise them.

The third is perhaps of greatest potential influence. The week before the publication of the PISA results of the 2015 tests, Andreas Schleicher (director of education and skills at the OECD) gave an interview with Helen Ward, a reporter from the *Times Educational Supplement* in the UK (Ward, 2016). He suggested in this interview that a significant aim of PISA is to share knowledge about the best way to educate children. It can offer information from which all can learn to improve.

> I think that when classroom doors are open – when schools know what other schools are doing and countries know what other countries are doing in a natural way – at that point, when the knowledge is mobilised, you won't need Pisa anymore.
>
> *(15)*

Schleicher likened PISA to a mirror to hold up to each country. He claimed it is not about seeing one country as superior to another. His insight, which offers the particular challenge of interest, cuts through the political imperatives that have formed much of the focus of this chapter. Schleicher raises the point that whilst the 72 countries participating in PISA in 2015 are looking at themselves in order to further develop (and compete), 'the future of our countries in Europe and the OECD depends a lot more on the education outside our borders than the education inside our borders' (15). Perhaps such a statement gives a strong steer to countries to think differently about the purpose of their education systems, both in and beyond their boundaries.

This chapter has focused on the pervading nature of the standards agenda and how it shapes policy and practice throughout education. In shaping the 'learning gap' between countries and against an international average, it reveals how such performance standards frame the learning gap to be addressed in classrooms. It sets limits, boundaries, and expectations for all pupils. Communication between teachers and pupils becomes increasing steered and determined by such policy narratives. Hence, feedback from teachers to pupils about their learning is increasingly caught

up in this standards agenda, and becomes more about striving for successful performance on external measures than about the immediate learning context in which
teaching and learning is experienced. In recognising the importance of this national
and international agenda, this book seeks to move beyond it. Attention is now
turned in the following chapters to social and individual considerations in the
process of feedback. It seeks to (re)conceptualise feedback in other ways. It does so
by identifying the learning gap, which feedback addresses, differently. In accordance with Tanner (2013: 9), 'No education reform can succeed if the curriculum
ignores or violates the psychosocial nature of the learner and the democratic
process.' It is to such issues that the focus now turns.

# 5

# CONCEPTUALISING THE LEARNING GAP

## A relational approach

### Chapter overview

Of significance in this chapter is the way in which the learning gap might be understood in terms of the relationship between the teacher and the pupil. This relational focus extends not only to the participants but also to the relationships between the processes of teaching and learning. In essence, the learning gap becomes more of a relational space in which pupils interact with others. Feedback becomes part of the communicative interaction in this space. The theoretical perspective here offers a marked shift from the previous chapter, which focused on a deterministic and instrumental view of teaching and learning. In this chapter, understandings about teaching and learning, and about teachers and pupils, are located within social constructivism. The focus provides not only the foundations for this chapter but develops the theoretical perspective upon which the remainder of the book is shaped. Particular attention is given to exploring Vygotsky's notion of the Zone of Proximal Development. The ZPD is a concept based on the construction of a 'gap' or zone which extends beyond existing learning and development, and requires interaction with a more knowledgeable other. It is explored within this chapter as a conceptual space in which feedback can be usefully understood and applied from a relational perspective.

### Social constructivism and social constructionism

Applied to a framework of understanding learning, social constructivism was developed from Piaget's theory of genetic epistemology. Piaget's theory of how knowledge is learnt was rooted in what he termed 'psychogenesis' (Piaget, 1972). This, Piaget considered, was the basis of interactions by the self-conscious developing learner with the objects in his/her environment. Learning was considered to be constructive, in the sense that it stemmed from 'the point of contact between the body itself and external things, they will develop in two complementary directions given by the external and internal' (1972: 20). However, in addition to being 'psychogenetic', he also suggested that it was 'biogenetic' in that he believed there were particular biologically determined stages. The basis of Piaget's constructivism, therefore, offers a theory in which understanding how knowledge is learnt, is determined by maturing and developing biological and psychological processes and an individual's engagement with his/her environment. Critique and development of Piaget's contribution, developed initially in the Russian school of psychology, was most notable through Vygotsky's (a student of Piaget's) consideration of the social influences on learning. Vygotsky's insight into the ways in which social interactions and contexts influence knowledge construction provided the starting point for the development of social constructivism. This recognised that the objective world, the developing and maturing being of the child, and his/her social environment all needed to be part of understanding teaching and learning.

In constructivism the learner is active and engaged in the way in which s/he constructs knowledge. The relationship with the world and those in it are significant to the process of learning and teaching. In the context of this chapter, the focus is on the learning gap being identified as part of this relationship. More explicitly, the focus is on how we can better understand the gap between learning now and its next steps, which in Vygotsky's theory will ultimately influence psychological development. Before we consider how the learning gap might be conceptualised further in terms of a relational approach, consideration on what is meant by being relational seems essential. Drawing on Vygotsky's seminal contribution to framing social constructivism is the idea that 'every function in the child's cultural development appears twice: first, on the social level, and later, on the individual level; first, between people (interpsychological) and then inside the child (intrapsychological)' (1978/1930: 57). Vygotsky clearly highlighted the child as intrinsically social, and argued that speech was far less specifically objectified into precise meanings than Piaget claimed. By acknowledging the importance of speech and language being socially and historically contextualised, Vygotsky shifted theoretical thinking about child development into what subsequently became a social constructivist perspective.

Influential also was the thinking of John Dewey who through his contribution in the writing of *Democracy and Education* (1916) and *Experience and Nature* (1929) shaped thinking about the nature of experience of education and the social context of teaching and learning. Subsequently, consideration of the role of language, experience, context and their interaction has been interlinked to explain how knowledge is socially constructed. Such notions extend beyond Vygotsky's work and have been developed more recently by social psychologists such as Wertsch (e.g. 1991) and Mercer (e.g. 1995). Within this chapter some of the neo Vygotskian perspectives are also briefly considered as part of framing an understanding of how a relational understanding of the learning gap may be insightful.

Distinctive to the developmental psychology in which Piaget and Vygotsky have their roots is a more broad-reaching theoretical perspective of social 'constructionism' within sociology. Berger and Luckmann (1966) drew together the philosophical roots and present what has developed into a major strand of understanding in sociology. Here, the focus is not specifically on an individual child's development but on the way in which knowledge, 'reality', is constructed. It takes us to the theoretical tension between positivism and interpretivism. Here, the question is of whether the world and our understanding of it is objective and measurable in scientific ways of exactitude, or whether reality is socially constructed and understanding is gained in far more complex and less precise ways of knowing. The distinction is significant in this book as the positioning of the child and his/her learning is recognised as being set in an educational world dominated by national prescription and measurement (see chapter 4). However, it is also recognised that the specific social and cultural influences for each child may be equally explored and exploited in an attempt to both understand and advance learning.

Within both social constructivism and social constructionism there is a clear emphasis on language having many layers of meaning and being more than the specific speech utterances that are physically formed and conveyed. Vygotsky (1962) offers in much detail how speech is far more than words, but has a complex link with thought, particularly through the development of 'inner speech' (130) and is socially and historically grounded. Vygotsky offers a particular understanding of inner speech which he defines as 'speech for oneself' (131). This offers a marked distinction from Piaget's understanding of speech for oneself, which Piaget (1972) frames as egocentric, and as part of the fundamental development of concepts of knowledge. Understanding the distinction between inner speech and egocentric speech, and its significance, will be clarified later in this chapter. The relationship between feedback and inner speech is developed at both the relational level between pupil and teacher and the individual level for pupils' own agency and development of their learning.

Learning is socially situated as it occurs 'somewhere'. In accepting such a view, the notion that learning is in some way relational (with its context) is also essential. Furthermore, there is recognition that the social context is embedded in a cultural history in which there is a past, a present and probably a future. Learning thus becomes relational in terms of its position in time as well as in how participants choose to emphasise and exclude elements of culture. In so doing they position themselves within it, by allowing others to dominate or influence it, or by seizing agency for themselves for personal positioning. Vygotsky clearly advances his view that learning is social. Through the use of cultural tools and symbols, which are culturally formed and embedded in both history and context, the child learns and develops. 'Through others, we become ourselves' (1978/1930: 30). Yet, Vygotsky does not advocate that learning is only a social process. He recognises that learning/teaching passes through the social but is eventually transformed by the learner and becomes uniquely individual.

Attention is now turned to exploring how the relationship between teaching and learning can be further understood within social constructivism. Vygotsky offers a particularly useful and insightful way of framing the learning relationship through his concept of the Zone of Proximal Development (ZPD). The extent to which this may add to our understanding of 'the gap' between learning and teaching is now given some consideration. Furthermore, the extent to which the learning gap may be considered to be relational within the ZPD forms a particular focus for this chapter.

## The Zone of Proximal Development

Vygotsky (1978/1930) draws attention to the need for learning to be understood as the interpretation of meaning and knowledge in context. He recognises both the internal cognitive processes of learning together with the social context of understanding meaning in a generalisable broad context, rather than in a specific singular way of deriving meaning. His discussion is centred on understanding child development, and his consideration of the ZPD is firmly rooted in a developmental model of maturation. He identified the ZPD as 'the distance between the actual developmental level as determined by independent problem solving and the level of potential development as determined through problem solving under adult guidance or in collaboration with more capable peers' (1978: 86). This examination of the ZPD is linked specifically to children as part of their development process. He makes a clear distinction between learning and development. However, Scrimsher and Tudge (2003: 298) highlight the need for some caution. The translated texts of Vygotsky's work into English do not consistently translate the original term '*obuchenie*' from the Russian. Early translations of Vygotsky's work *Thought and Language* and *Mind and Society*, which still tend to dominate, tend to translate the term as 'learning'. Later translations, with a more accurate translated title of *Thinking and Speech* translate the word as 'instruction'. Thus, issues of translation create some tensions and confusion when seeking to understand the notions of teaching and learning, and particularly their interaction. The difficulties in translation convey something of what is thought to be Vygotsky's intended meaning. That is, that teaching and learning are to interrelate and that the terminology virtually merges into one word. The English language is therefore unhelpful, as it does not include a suitable single word to embrace the complex interrelation between teaching and learning. Scrimsher and Tudge, in drawing attention to the need for a more nuanced and considered understanding of Vygotsky's meaning for teaching and learning, suggest that you learn best when you teach and that teachers teach best whilst they are learning (298).

For Vygotsky, there is an important relationship between learning and teaching, as well as between teaching/learning and development. This is well exemplified through the following statement: 'The zone of proximal development – which determines the domain of transitions that are accessible to the child – is a defining feature of the relationship between (teaching/learning) and development' (Vygotsky 1987/1934: 211).

The development process thus lags behind the teaching/learning processes. As a starting point, Vygotsky ponders how two children who are identified as being at the same level of development might achieve quite different levels if they are offered specific support to move beyond their current stage of development. Vygotsky realised that, even from the same starting point, when children were supported by a more capable 'other' they might respond in different ways and thus move forward to different extents from the support they receive. Of significance for Vygotsky is that although actual development, determined 'retrospectively' through a pupil's independent problem solving is important, more important is how learning/teaching and development are considered 'prospectively' (1978: 86). Vygotsky contextualises the ZPD as being within

> functions that have not matured yet, but are in the process of maturing, that will mature tomorrow, that are currently in an embryonic state; these functions could be called the buds of development, rather than the fruits of development, that is, what is only just maturing.
>
> *(Vygotsky, 1978/1930: 86)*

Vygotksy's contribution of the notion of ZPD has featured prominently in education for nearly a century. From the definitions already given, some thought into how his theory may help us understand and frame both teaching and learning is offered. Its significance in this book is the way it seeks to explain and frame a learning gap. Yet, it is important to highlight a few caveats. The translated works of Vygotsky are problematic, as many of the ideas and notions inherent in the research field derive from the early translations of *Thought and Language* and *Mind in Society*, both of which are truncated translations and often considered distorted portrayals of Vygotsky's work (Gillen, 2000). Vygotsky's notion of ZPD, in particular, is not so much considered to be distorted in the line of translation and application but over used and given greater prominence than Vygotsky may have intended. Application of the ZPD has often been used as a generalised theory for identifying how teachers enable and scaffold pupil learning (Chaiklin, 2003). In a similar vein, Mercer and Fisher (1992) identify that it is often used as a fashionable way of explaining pupil differences, whereas Palincsar (1998) points to the use of ZPD and the emphasis on the negotiated and collaborative aspects of teaching and learning being the least understood construct in educational literature. Part of the aim of the consideration in this chapter is to make sense of how Vygotsky's thinking about the ZPD can be helpful in making sense of the learning gap – the gap between actual learning and future learning, which subsequently contributes to our understanding of feedback.

Chaiklin (2003: 42–43) sets out and critiques some of the assumptions that seem to characterise accepted understandings of Vygotsky's notion of the learning gap conceptualised through his notion of the ZPD

1. *'Generality assumption'* – the fact that Vygotsky has created the notion of Zone of Proximal Development rather than a zone of proximal learning, reflects the distinction that Vygotsky makes between development and teaching/learning. Although the two are related, learning/teaching are ahead of development,

and the way in which teaching and learning may translate into development will be unique for each child.

2.   *'Assistance assumption'* – since the notion of ZPD identifies the importance of a more capable 'other' there are assumptions associated with a view that what is important is the capability and competence of the 'other'. However, what is of greater importance is the relationship which seeks to understand meanings within the ZPD.

3.   *'Potential assumption'* – the view that the potential for learning is the property of the child (or the teacher) is inaccurate. It is merely an indication that developmentally the child is maturing.

Recognising what the ZPD is, as well as what it is not, also requires greater understanding of why Vygotsky formulated this concept. Its foundation in child development was crucial and perhaps often lost in the popularisation of his work. Also, his concern for forming a theoretical basis for teaching/instruction was also essential. It is perhaps in this context that seeking the foundations for the ways of understanding this particular framing of a 'learning gap' within the overall focus of this book is important. If we are to piece together what sense we can make of the way learning develops and the ways in which teachers and learners fit into this processes then probing beneath the surface is paramount.

All too often Vygotsky's contribution to understanding teaching and learning, particularly, through his notion of the ZPD, has been overgeneralised. Scrimsher and Tudge (2003) offer helpful insight here in pointing out that the ZPD is not

> some clear cut space that exists independently of the process of joint activity, despite the fact that many authors write as though the teacher's role is to identify the space between what the child currently knows and what the teacher can help them to know.
>
> *(Scrimsher and Tudge, 2003: 300)*

This is an important point to consider and immediately sets a tension between this view of the learning gap and the more deterministic picture portrayed in the previous chapter in which control is external to the learner. What Vygotsky offers for consideration is summarised below to enable a more focused account of his contribution. Main features of the ZPD include:

1.   Development can be identified as an actual level of performance but beyond this lies a zone in which learning/teaching can occur with help from others, which may eventually result in future development

2.   What a child can do with help may eventually become tomorrow's development, but this developmental step is identified by Vygotsky as an internal process. 'Every function in the child's cultural development appears twice: first, on the social level, and later, on the individual level; first, between people (interpsychological) and then inside the child (intrapsychological). This

applies equally to voluntary attention, to logical memory, and to the formation of concepts. All the higher functions originate as actual relationships between individuals' (Vygotsky, 1978/1930: 57). He thus seemingly advances a distinction between collaborative endeavours and personal internal thinking.

3. Vygotsky recognises that after actual levels of development are determined the ways in which pupils may advance will vary. This implies that it is not so much the teaching techniques and collaborations that determine the differences in next steps in learning or development, but issues related to personal traits, inner thinking, as well as personal histories and experiences of the culture and tools of learning being used.

4. The relationship between teaching and learning is central to Vygotsky's notion of ZPD. It is a collaborative relationship that is bi-directional, rather than a unidirectional process in which the teacher identifies and co-constructs learning.

5. The context in which Vygotsky considers and discusses ZPD is not as a general all-embracing theoretical notion to his work, but he presents it in two specific contexts: play and assessment.

In establishing what the ZPD is conceptually, there are some further nuances to consider. Vygotsky considered that certain zone of proximal developments would be required during an age period which would move the child through to a new period of development. Chaiklin (2003) defines these as the '*objective*' ZPD: 'One could say that the zone for a given period is normative, in that it reflects the institutionalized demands and expectations that developed historically in a particular societal tradition of practice' (47). He also identified a '*subjective*' zone of proximal development. This 'subjective' ZPD is typically the zone that we most closely focus on when considering Vygotsky. It refers to the zone beyond actual development, when, with another, a child can demonstrate more than s/he can alone. Chaiklin therefore points out that the whole notion of the ZPD includes recognition of development that has already matured, as well as the maturing functions that with the help of another, will ultimately move the child on to the next level of development.

What becomes important is how Vygotsky sees what happens in the subjective zone, which ultimately has an impact on development. Two particular strands are therefore crucial here. Firstly, how do we define the ZPD? Secondly, what happens within it so that learning and subsequently development can advance? These will both be given some consideration. Some of the more recent translations of Vygotsky's work offer more insights than his early previously translated texts. However, unfortunately his explanations are far from crisp.

## Identifying the Zone of Proximal Development

Looking at the origins of Vygotsky's thinking on the framing and application of the ZPD, it is clear that initial references were linked to alternative ways to understand the measurement of intelligence. This was partly connected to his desire to understand children whose development had not advanced in expected ways. Common practice, in the Soviet context of the time, was to give all children entering elementary school an intelligence test. On this basis children were allocated to different categories of school. However, as van der Veer and Valsiner (1991) point out, there was an additionally observed phenomenon, that once at school, differences in initial IQ regressed towards the mean. Thus, the impact of schooling varied for different children using these IQ measurements. Vygotsky argued that measurements of actual development provided only a limited glimpse into pupils' learning and potential learning. Examining the extent to which children could learn when given prompts and questions by more capable others provided a different way of looking at learning. Vygotsky, in identifying that some children, from the same actual starting point, could achieve more when helped than others, revealed a new way of looking at learning potential. He claimed that understanding learning in two ways, actual and supported, was vital within the context of schooling. Vygotsky was, in fact, changing understandings of diagnosing children's developmental levels of achievement. In the context of formal schooling, knowing the absolute level of development within a continual process of maturation, was of little value (even if possible). For Vygotsky, changing the meaning of development in a school context, away from a snap shot in a moment of time, to gaining an understanding of future learning, was crucial. 'A true diagnosis must provide an explanation, prediction, and scientific basis for practical prescription' (Vygotsky, 1998/1934: 205).

Vygotsky's emphasis was on discerning the parameters of the ZPD. He claims,

> it remains necessary to determine the lowest threshold at which instruction in, say, arithmetic may begin since a certain minimal ripeness of functions is required. But we must consider the upper threshold as well; instruction must be orientated toward the future, not the past.
>
> *(Vygotsky, 1962: 104)*

Therefore, it seems imperative that teachers establish what a child can do unaided and what s/he cannot do. Although Vygotsky recognises that certain age-related psychological functions can be usefully understood in order to help diagnosis, there is also the need to seek out the extent of their ZPD. Vygotsky recognised that children's understanding of their 'everyday concepts' will also have an impact on the sense they make of school 'scientific concepts'. Hence, the ways in which children learn and the size of their ZPD is not solely determined by age-related norms or external structured instruction.

Vygotsky's concerns with schooling were brought centre stage in the final years of his life. His writing of the sixth chapter of *Thinking and Speech* (initially translated as *Thought and Language*) about the development of 'scientific concepts' (formal taught concepts as distinct from ones the child learns 'every day' out of school) seem likely to have been undertaken very near to his death in the summer of 1934 at the age of 37. Following a series of six lectures in Leningrad and some manuscripts gathered after his death (van der Veer and Valsiner, 1991: 328), he began to more specifically present his ideas about the relationship between teaching and cognitive development. The Zone of Proximal Development increasingly seemed to offer an explanation for his ideas on the role of schooling and for the teacher.

## Interactions within the ZPD

Specific details of how learning should progress within the ZPD, or what exactly the teacher (or more capable other) must do to maximise learning, and subsequently development, was not clear. Presumably, this was his work in progress and his untimely death has resulted in others trying to seize his ideas and principles and develop them further. There are some brief glimpses. In *Thought and Language* (1962: 107) Vygotsky asks why, in a particular example, a child seems to be able to give an answer beyond his immediate level of achievement. Vygotsky states in response: 'because the teacher working with the pupil, has explained, supplied information, questioned, corrected and made the pupil explain' (107). There are a number of pedagogical devices suggested here which, although include giving information also include bi-directional interactions. Furthermore, Vygotsky clearly indicates how psychological tools (sometimes called tools and signs) are used by the teacher in the process of mediated action. He exemplifies these as 'language; various systems for counting; mnemonic techniques; algebraic symbol systems; works of art; writing; schemes, diagrams, maps, and mechanical drawings; all sorts of conventional signs and so on' (1981: 157).

Implicit in his notion of what happens in the ZPD are a number of dimensions to the teacher's role within classroom pedagogy. Furthermore, he highlights that it is not entirely focused on what the teacher does, but also includes the actions, contributions and thinking of the pupil.

Mercer (2000: 141) develops Vygotsky's work a little in exploring the processes within the ZPD. The interactive social processes that Vygotsky characterises as the interpsychological plane are considered in more detail by Mercer (following Minick's (in Vygotsky, 1987) translation of intermental in place of interpsychological). Mercer promotes the idea of a shared space for language and activity and he suggests that this space within the ZPD is called the intermental development zone (IDZ). For Littleton and Mercer (2013: 111), this IDZ is maintained through dialogue. If the dialogue fails to 'keep minds mutually attuned' the zone collapses. Littleton and Mercer claim that his suggestion of the IDZ is a more nuanced articulation of the ZPD. 'The IDZ is a continuing event of contextualised joint activity, whose quality is dependent on the existing knowledge, capabilities and motivations of both the learner and the teacher' (141). The shift in focus and emphasis to a more specific role for dialogue is an area for further discussion within this book. However, it strays a little from Vygotsky's offering, which will remain the focus for a little longer.

Vygotsky is quite limited in how he explains the relationships within the ZPD. However, he promotes two key strands of imitation and activity. These enable further understanding of Vygotsky's thinking of the functioning and relationships within the ZPD.

## Imitation within the ZPD

Understanding the notion of imitation within Vygotsky's theory is treated with some caution. The terminology that Vygotsky chose to use may well be understood quite differently in our twenty-first-century understandings of learning and pedagogy. Vygotsky's technical translation of the ZPD into practice centred on the notion of 'imitation'. Vygotsky was himself clear that there were other uses and understandings of the term so he deliberately tried to give clear indication of what he meant. In making comparisons with animals, he identified it was certainly not about copying in a mechanical way, rather it was about 'insightful solutions' (1962: 104). Van der Veer and Valsiner (1991) highlight that Vygotsky was referring to 'intellectual imitation' (343). Additionally, Vygotsky includes the notion of play within the ZPD, which includes elements of imitation that children interpret, extend and develop.

Vygotsky's use of the term 'imitation' is about the way the child is able to interact with another so that s/he can do more than s/he can do alone. Vygotsky thought that 'there is a strict genetic pattern between what a child is able to imitate and his mental development' (1987: 202). For Vygotsky this highlights and reinforces the notion of the ZPD having parameters within which the child can interact. Imitation is part of this interaction requiring some understanding on the part of the child of the structures of the problem or learning being encountered, which is an aspect of the collaborative encounter (1987: 202).

## Activity within the ZPD

In understanding Vygotsky there is a very clear distinction made between how learning happens which is specifically compared with previous structured predetermined approaches (considered in the previous chapter). Whereas in previous theoretical perspectives the important components within understanding learning were the learner and the environment, for Vygotsky a third element is critically included. That is the 'activity' that occurs in the relation between the two. With our focus on the ZPD, this is crucial in how learning is about active engagement with both people and the environment. Vygotsky is vehement in his criticism of teachers merely communicating information to be learnt by pupils. In Vygotsky's view such an approach leads to 'nothing more than simulation and imitation of corresponding concepts which, in reality, are concealing a vacuum. In such cases, the child assimilates not concepts but words, and he fills his memory rather than his thinking' (Vygotsky, 1934, in van der Veer and Valsiner, 1994: 356). The essential component of activity has been further developed after Vygotsky's death. Leontiev (1978), a student of Vygotsky, is perhaps the most notable for furthering the foundational position of activity in socio-cultural theory. He promotes the idea that an individual's activity is central within the social relations in which he may engage. Furthermore, he claims, such activities are influenced by the goals, opportunities and constraints which influence each person.

What is most significant here is trying to establish not only what the ZPD is but how it might account for framing the learning gap between what is known now to what is known next. Vygotsky's notion of the ZPD includes actively engaging processes in which the learner, together with another, interact in order to move forwards with learning. It recognises that both the learner and the more capable other are changed in the processes. This has distinctive implications for how the process of feedback might feature as part of learning and development. It requires that the ways in which next steps might be understood and learning advanced are recognised as part of a bi-directional process. These next steps need to be formed collaboratively, and be sensitive to the cultural and environmental interpretations and experiences of both parties. By exploring more specifically how feedback might operate in the social relational world of activity, it is intended that our understanding of learning and the role of feedback will be further enhanced. However, our understanding of how learning advances within the ZPD is not yet complete. A further dimension to understand in Vygotsky's theory, having addressed the interpsychological level (between people), must also consider the intrapsychological (internal thinking).

## The intrapsychological process

The interaction with a more capable other within the ZPD is only one part of a learning process. The second dimension, which may influence development, concerns the way the child internalises what s/he has experienced. It is important to note that Vygotsky is not advocating a simple transformative process from the external to the internal plane in some kind of linear event. Rather, he talks of 'a constant interaction between outer and inner operations, one form effortlessly and frequently changing into the other and back again' (1962: 47). Speech and language are crucial at both levels. Clearly, the interaction with another person forms part of this socially constructed learning encounter. Within the interpsychological plane such language is for others and is regarded as social. However, the second level of internalising learning is a matter for what Vygotsky calls inner speech. Vygotsky (1962) identifies inner speech as 'speech for oneself' (131), and it therefore has a different function. Vygotsky draws some parallels with egocentric speech in young children in Piaget's theory. However, he identifies that it is not just speech without sound, but an entirely separate type of speech being 'disconnected and incomplete' (1962: 139). Vygotsky claims that inner speech has a reduced numbers of words, almost to the point of having no words at all. What dominates and remains is the 'sense' of key words, rather than their meanings. Thus, he claims inner speech 'works with semantics, not phonetics' (1962: 145).

Despite having few words, he claims inner speech still remains speech, which he highlights as being the connection between thought and word. Inner speech has more thought than words whereas external speech has more words (149). Vygotsky therefore considers inner speech to be syntactically reduced, using abbreviations, removing the 'subject' and associated words, but preserving the predicate. Furthermore, he identifies it as particularly semantic, preserving the contextual sense of words. Even though this speech is directed at the self, it is still intrinsically social in that the sense it conveys maintains its historical, cultural and social influences.

The importance of speech, which together with other cultural tools form the foundation for the way in which individuals mediate their actions within their particular context, is vital to understand. Thus, in the classroom, both the pupil and more capable other use tools and signs as part of their collaboration within the ZPD. Speech plays its part at both the interpsychological and intrapsychological levels. At both levels its semantics are crucial. Even when used as inner speech, Vygotsky claims that its social context and sense prevail. Vygotsky's consideration of inner speech (intrapsychological plane) is less clearly articulated than his ideas related to the interpsychological plane. Undoubtedly, this will relate to the relative inaccessibility of hearing inner speech. Yet, it is important to the theory he develops. It is the internalisation through the intraspsychological plane that enables development to advance following learning. Furthermore, as Wertsch (1991) illuminates, Vygotsky, just before his death, was beginning to give more specific thought to identifying 'historically, culturally, and institutionally situated forms of mediated action and specify how their mastery leads to particular forms of mediated action on the intramental plane' (48). (Note: Wertsch, 1991: 26 draws on Minick's translation using the terms 'intermental and intramental'.)

What can be surmised about inner speech is that although it may happen at an individual level (i.e. without others physically being present), its processes are still historically, culturally and socially influenced. Together across both planes, Vygotsky's consideration of the form and function of speech and language is essential. Before drawing together the implications for the classroom some further consideration of speech and language is offered as it is pivotal for understanding Vygotsky and for the relational dimensions being explored.

## The significance of language and speech within social constructivism for feedback

The link between language and thought is at the centre of Vygotsky's theory. It forms the foundation for classroom interaction. Clearly, in the context of this book, feedback is a particular process centred on language. If often includes codes and symbols which represent meanings about what is good, and what requires further work. It assumes shared meanings, and is often tightly structured by the teacher to target particular learning outcomes. However, Vygotsky clearly identifies that language is historically, culturally and contextually located for *all* participants. Thus, the ways in which language may be both formed and understood varies within the teaching/learning relationship of the ZPD. The relational context formed here is one in which particular learning, and hopefully development, will occur. Therefore, it is not a question of each individual forming a completely unique and separate trajectory in their learning. Although their experiences and socio-cultural backgrounds will be evident, there is some notion that rather than there being no shared meanings, that there is a process of co-construction in which these differences can be shared and negotiated. This recognition forms a fundamental difference between a relationship that is dialectic rather than dialogic. (This needs further exploration and is discussed in chapter 8.)

At this point, just a brief explanation of the distinction between dialogic and dialectic language relationships is considered. Although Vygotsky is often associated with a dialogic approach to learning in socio-cultural theory, he offers virtually no use of the term dialogue. In *Thought and Language* (1962), or its more recent translation *Thinking and Speech*, Vygotsky gives a little insight to his thinking about dialogic speech. He claims that written and inner speech tend to be a monologue, and oral speech a dialogue (142). He then acknowledges that dialogue tends to be the natural form of speech, but that monologue is a higher and more complicated form (144). Additionally, and more importantly within the focus of this book, he identifies that dialogue is immediate as it 'consists of replies, repartee; it is a chain of reactions. Monologue, by comparison, is a complex formation; the linguistic elaboration can be attended to leisurely and consciously' (144).

Within Vygotsky's writings there are much stronger references to his Hegelian roots. Vygotsky himself states that his developmental approach is part of his contribution to a Hegelian dialectic. Here, there is greater recognition that individuals bring different perspectives and there is a coming together (co-construction) to overcome the differences. He illustrates how the use of cultural tools is applied to higher mental faculties. For Vygotsky, building on Piaget's theory, he had some notion of stable periods of development as well as shared aspects of development that form in the development process. This draws a distinction with a dialogic approach in which meanings cannot be related to fixed and stable aspects of development, and there is a greater recognition of differences with multiple voices remaining from dialogue. Although Vygotsky advocated that his contributions to understanding psychological development were dialectical, these related to structures and some form of development leading towards a unified whole. Furthermore, the structures which he presents have been insufficient to equate to a theory with a transformative methodology (van der Veer and Valsiner, 1991: 180 and 398). Nevertheless, he does offer a process for dialectical synthesis that would help explain the progress of development.

## The learning gap as relational

Exploration of the learning gap in this chapter has centred on Vygotsky's notion of the Zone of Proximal Development. Its focus is on what learners can accomplish with a more capable 'other' rather than alone. It highlights the bi-directional relationship between at least two people, in which signs and tools are used to mediate learning. Such learning is related to existing development, but lies beyond established development using psychological functions that are not yet mature. There is an assumption that meanings and interpretations will be different as each person is socially, culturally and contextually influenced in different ways, and that all participants will be changed through their learning encounters. Speech and language are important in two ways. Firstly, between people as it is used in the interpsychological plane, and secondly, as a form of inner speech in the intrapsychological plane, which is used by each learner in order to internalise new ways of thinking. In both processes the meaning of speech is seen in social, historical and contextual terms, rather than as received information.

When considering school contexts, it is clear from Vygotsky's theory that individual children will relate differently to what is being taught. Each child will appropriate the knowledge forms on offer according to their own interpretations and connections made to their own existing development. Newman et al. (1989) offer a useful insight, 'there is no assumption that all parties involved in the ZPD have the *same* notion of what is going to happen' (64). They highlight that within the ZPD there is no simple process of mapping out what a child is offered within the ZPD against what a child ultimately learns. What is apparent is that learning and development are actively constructed within the ZPD through the complex processes of inter and intra psychological process. There is scope for pupils' learning to be structured and shaped by more capable others, yet ultimate recognition is given to the pupil interaction in the processes of co-constructing learning. In Holland et al.'s (1998: 272) words, the ZPD provides the space for self authoring, a space in which voices and interpretations can be assembled.

Newman et al. (1989) draw on the phrase 'dialogue with the child's future' (64) to illustrate the processes within the ZPD. This certainly highlights the importance of the process being projective and seeking to move learning forward, pushing beyond actual development in a socially communicative framework. Yet, it may not quite fit completely with Vygotsky's positioning within dialectics. However, Vygotsky is clear to frame an important space in which a learner and another have a relationship, in which meanings are explored and shared, and which ultimately enable development to advance for all participants. Vygotsky identifies this space as having upper and lower boundaries, yet also offers a sense in which these shift as what is initially interpsychological is internalised.

Vygotsky's notion of the ZPD forms a useful understanding of the learning gap. Understanding the relationship between teaching and learning in more particular and complex ways may help the development and use of feedback. If feedback processes are to enable learning to progress, in order to close (or alter) the learning gap, gaining greater insight into what this gap is and how it is constructed, maintained and developed merits the careful attention offered in this chapter. There are some key issues that emerge from the analysis so far, that have implications for the type of feedback that might be developed as part of our understanding of a relational understanding of the learning gap.

## Implications of a relational understanding of the learning gap for pupil feedback

Particular foundational issues can be teased out in this chapter, which will help frame feedback. These are highlighted below.

- The language of feedback must be shared and interpreted together (pupil and teacher/more capable other).
- Each participant has a role in forming, shaping and assimilating feedback.
- Feedback about an activity and/or imitation not only comments on the past, but projects into the future – highlighting a relationship between time frames.
- There should be recognition that understanding of the structures and systems of the learning environment, including tools and signs, will not be seen in the same way by the teacher and pupil – this should be explored and revealed not suppressed.
- Feedback contains language that is social and shared – a 'language for others'.
- Feedback needs to feed into inner speech, which will enable new thinking and connections – indicating a relationship of shared speech with inner speech.
- Even at the point when feedback is being internalised (through inner speech) different voices (perspectives) may still remain.
- Feedback is part of the teaching/learning relationship rather than an isolated one-directional judgement or set of instructions.
- Action, resulting from feedback, is also part of the continued process of mediated action, not a passive process of reading or hearing.

This chapter has sought to understand the learning gap as a relational space. It has done so by using Vygotsky's notion of the ZPD as an anchor for explanation, and a context for framing the relationship of teaching and learning (teacher and pupil). Although it is recognised that the idea of the ZPD is not fully developed and has been subject to critique, enhancement and applications, it does provide a way of understanding a learning and teaching space. Seeking to understand how feedback might be a mediating and cultural tool in such conceptualising offers a different account of what feedback might do and how it might be enacted. This contrasts with the more deficit defining constructions of the learning gap in the previous chapter. It adds another distinctive layer to making sense of feedback. The following chapter adds a further conceptual layer, which tightens the focus further. It considers how feedback must relate to learners' individual experiences of education.

# 6

# CONCEPTUALISING THE LEARNING GAP

## An individualistic approach

### Chapter overview

In seeking to understand how the learning gap may be altered, particular concern needs to be given to the individual within the experience of education. In chapter 4 the phrase the 'learning gap' was explored in its national and international policy context. This was revealed through the comparisons of results between countries, as well as nationally and at school level, between groups of children. Such groups included those who are on free school meals and those who are not, boys and girls, all identified from schools and national pupil performance data. In chapter 5 the learning gap was examined in a socio-cultural context, through inter-personal relational encounters in which each child's learning gap shifts through the active interaction of teaching and learning, of which feedback is a part. The focus in this chapter is on individual pupils and their experiences of education. It considers how the uniqueness of each pupil brings a very personal dimension to understanding education. Each child's uniqueness may also be culturally and socially shaped, but remains distinctive within the educational encounter.

Feedback is used as a way in which the pupil positions him/herself in the education process and projects a pathway within it. This pathway is steered and controlled in complex ways, influenced by teachers and school context but also driven by each pupil. Some of the mechanisms that children use to control their learning were explored in chapter 2 through concepts such as self-regulation, meta-learning and metacognition. These are certainly part of an individualistic approach, but focus more sharply on the mechanism of learning and understanding the learning gap in a cognitive sense.

The focus in this chapter is more specific, and although linked to some extent to the cognitive process of learning, is also socially situated. It considers a more personal, and in some ways a more emotional response to learning. Recognition is given to an essential understanding that learning must relate to, and be part of, the learner. Thus, this chapter offers an additional interpretation and perspective on how we need to understand the learning gap as well as considering how feedback is used. This extends what might be considered an individualistic approach to learning to a deliberately broader notion, beyond cognition. Its particular focus is on how pupils are able to think about possible learning futures, and have curiosity to engage with new learning.

## Locating the pupil in the educational endeavour

It might be thought that an individualistic approach is akin to a child-centred approach giving control to the learner who pursues his/her own idea of education with no structure, focus or discipline. Such a view is not being advocated here. Even Freire (1998: 83), often regarded as an influential proponent of child-centred education, acknowledges a 'tense harmony between freedom and authority'. Rather, the focus is on recognising that the pupil is not merely the commodity and out-come of the process of education, but is a unique individual who will shape and experience education in particular ways. The teacher and the curriculum are not regarded as the sole influences on learning. Both the teacher and curriculum are recognised as important within both policy and practice as part of formal schooling. What seems crucial and embraced in this chapter, is that pupils have significant control over their engagement with, and outcomes of, learning. It seems that despite unyielding attempts to tighten the process of education, so that outcomes might become more uniform and tighter, this is not quite so straight forward. As the discussion in chapter 4 outlined, the intensification of the curriculum and assessment practices, in an attempt to raise standards, seems to miss two funda-mental considerations – the purpose of education beyond economic production and the active curiosity of pupils in their learning.

## Recognising learning beyond economic outcomes

Biesta (2006) offers significant insight into the limitations of current policy prio-rities. He critiques the over emphasis on learning in contemporary educational policy. That is a particular type of learning that pervades the whole of education promoting learning as 'economic transaction' (19). He calls this 'learnification' (2010). Pupils are moulded as learners to produce a certain type of learning, measured in particular ways. In this interpretation, the process of learning is not particularly important, just the outcomes. This is certainly echoed in the 2016 White Paper – *Educational Excellence Everywhere* (DfE, 2016), which clearly states that 'outcomes matter more than methods, and that there is rarely one standardised solution that will work in every classroom for government to impose' (para 1.17) As Biesta contends, little consideration is given to the purpose of education beyond economic issues, nor is there is a broader under-standing of how education relates to the unique humanness of pupils. He calls for recognition that education should involve a language of education, rather than merely a focus on learning outcomes.

> Education is not just about the transmission of knowledge, skills and values, but is concerned with the individuality, subjectivity, or personhood of the student, with their 'coming into the world' as unique, singular beings.
>
> *(Biesta, 2006: 27)*

In this sense, the focus on an individualistic approach in this chapter seeks to understand the person in the process and experience of education. Even though contemporary policy (in England) highlights the importance of all children learning to their full potential, wherever they live and whatever their background (DfE, 2016: para 1.20), there is a clear sense in which this is promoted through a more standardised, collective, evidence-based approach. The White Paper (DfE, 2016) points to this issue and advocates that new teachers entering the profession must have 'the most up-to-date research on how pupils learn' (para 1.36c). Furthermore, the Education Endowment Foundation was set up by the UK government to support research that would offer robust evidence on the best strategies for teaching and learning. The meta-analysis available for all teachers to access, reduced a wide range of possible strategies to an 'effect size' (as discussed in chapter 3). Thus, offering a simple score, which is intended to help teachers select the most effective practices to adopt in their classroom, aimed at standardised notions of pupil learning.

Although the research from the Educational Endowment Foundation (EEF) is a useful resource in some sense, it has to be understood in terms of what it is, and how it might be used by teachers. For example, feedback is illustrated as being low in cost, supported by a reasonable body of evidence, and through the processes of meta-analysis is identified as having a very high effect size (+ 8 months). This certainly points teachers in the direction of giving careful consideration to using feedback, but as Wiliam (2016) points out, it does not show how feedback might best serve particular pupils or groups of pupils and on what occasions.

This chapter focuses on the individual for a very important reason. Learning cannot simply be achieved through national policy, global testing, government dictate or the sheer brilliance of teaching. It is experienced and achieved by each learner through personal experience in particular contexts. Thus, what might be helpfully determined through large-scale random control trials, which do not seek to account for individual differences, offers only a glimpse of possibilities. It is how such possibilities might be shaped, formed, adapted and transformed for and by unique individuals that will gain the best outcomes in real classrooms.

## The limits of standardising individuals in research

Rose (2016: 1–4) offers a poignant illustration of the limitations of such mass standardised evidence and the dangers of its use. In the 1940s, the United States

Airforce experienced a large number of unexplained air accidents. These were not due to mechanical failure. At its worst there were 17 unexplained crashes in one day. As an investigation was launched, the possibility that the cockpit was no longer suitable for the new generation of pilots was raised. The original cockpit was designed in 1926 and based on the average measurements of hundreds of US pilots, and the cockpit design was based on these standardised measurements. The Airforce commissioned a new study in the 1950s, sampling 4,063 pilots on 140 different dimensions. Gilbert Daniels, a graduate in physical anthropology from Harvard, was part of the research team. He was sceptical as to whether findings from a new set of figures, averaging physical dimensions, would be useful.

He looked at the ten most important dimensions needed for identifying the 'average pilot' for cockpit design. He calculated the average dimensions for all 4,063 pilots in the sample. Once he determined the average measurement he identified a middle 30 per cent range of measurements around the average. So, if the average height were five foot nine, he selected the average pilot to be between five foot seven and five foot eleven. Daniels then decided to see how many of the 4,063 pilots matched the new 'average pilot' dimensions on all ten measurements (within the 30 per cent range). Daniels' results stunned everyone. There were no pilots matching the average pilot measurements in the ten measured areas. Even when only three measurements were selected, less than 3.5 per cent of pilots fitted the measured average in all three dimensions. What the study revealed was that 'there was no such thing as an average pilot' (Rose, 2016: 4).

Mass statistical results, which have lived most comfortably in the medical sciences, and have been carefully planted into education (Goldacre, 2009 and 2013), are certainly established in government education policy. However, as education promotes such a medical model of research and evidence, medical research has increasingly been recognising the importance of the uniqueness of the individual in treating and preventing illness. The Human Genome Research Institute advocates a personalised approach to medicine by including an 'individual's genetic profile to guide decisions made in regard to the prevention, diagnosis and treatment of disease' (McMullan, online). This is a growing global area for development, illustrated through the priority given to 'Precision Medicine' in President Obama's 2015 State of the Union Address (Obama, 2015a).

## Feedback within personal narrative

With a renewed emphasis on the importance of the individual and his/her uniqueness, further exploration, in the remainder of this chapter, is on additional factors which prioritie the individuality of pupils as learners. Of particular significance is the way in which each pupil develops his/her own narrative for the purpose of sense-making. Bruner (1990: 43) argues for recognition that each individual makes meaning in their own way. He identifies narrative (one's own story) which is personally sequenced and interpreted as key to understanding how we make meaning. This makes sense when considering learning. It requires consideration of how an individual narrates themselves as a learner within their own personal narrative of who they are and what they do. Bruner argues that in some sense there is a notion of 'a plot' in the sequencing of different (and perhaps competing narratives) for each individual. This personal sequencing of experiences is set alongside what Holland et al. (1998: 51) identify as the notion of the 'standard plot' which depicts agreed and established sequences that are part of convention, or in Bruner's terms, part of the 'canonical' (1990: 50). The ways in which an individual makes sense of his own experiences and sequences them seems to have a bearing on how they use the narrative of feedback as part of this personal narrative. Bruner claims 'people do not deal with the world event by event or with text sentence by sentence. They frame events and sentences in larger structures' (1990: 64). Thus, any message that feedback seeks to convey must be personally incorporated into large structures and sequences by the individual acting on it. The feedback can no longer remain as an external message. There must be an 'inward turn' (Bruner, 1990: 51) when the feedback becomes incorporated into the sequences and structures which the individual already has in place, only then it can be of use and of relevance.

When feedback is given, if it is seen as something that needs to become part of a narrativised process, acted on inwardly by each recipient, then it cannot be left as a factual standalone message. This links back to the previous chapter in which as well as being personal, feedback requires a relational aspect that recognises that the feedback message needs to be discussed from the differing perspectives of its participants. Its place and form within a sequence in an individual narrative will be very different. For the teacher, the feedback is certainly likely to be part of a 'standard plot' which is framed by standards and a particular set of professional expectations. For the recipient, although there may be intentions to convey a particular message related to a particular plot, conceived and legitimised by the educational system, its place in a personalised narrative may be very different.

The place and priority that feedback messages have for any individual are likely to relate to personal interest and a drive to engage in new learning. Thus not only is the 'inward turn' of the feedback important, and the way it fits into existing structures and sequences, but the priority it is given. These in some way relate to an individual's eagerness to seek out new learning.

Within the Teachers' Standards for all teachers in England, there is a statement which all teachers need to demonstrate – 'promote a love of learning and intellectual curiosity' (DfE, 2012a: standard 4b). Here, the ideas that children need to love learning and be curious to seek out new learning are embedded in the standards for all teachers. This highlights something additional to curriculum content that is important in the education process. Even though, within these teaching standards, there is a clear notion that teachers are able to promote a love of learning and intellectual curiosity, its occurrence points to something additional to knowledge that affects and influences the learning experience. It points to something that is contained within each individual child that influences his/her experience in education.

Gaining a greater grasp of what might be meant within this policy context has been of particular interest in recent years (Dann, 2013). It provides a particularly useful legitimate pathway to exploring the individual within the process and experience of education. How curiosity is understood, frames a pupil's learning experience, becomes part of the learning gap between what is known now and next, and partly defines how feedback might be sought and used. This is further explored in this chapter.

## Being curious

Learning is not a passive process, as the previous chapter illuminated. The notion of curiosity is not easily reduced to something tangible and measurable. Thus, robust evidence of what it is and what it can do defy easy articulation. My best recourse is to a story reported in national newspapers in England in March 2016. It is about a boy named Toby Little, who at the age of five was talking to his mum as he walked home from school clutching his newly borrowed book *Letter to New Zealand*, written by the children's author Alison Hawes. The book was about the journey a letter makes once posted, travelling from one side of the world to the other. As Toby walked home with his mum he asked if he could write a letter to New Zealand. A few steps later Toby asked, 'Can I write letters to every country in the world?' His mum agreed. His mum was reported as saying, 'It was just one of those typical questions that five-year-olds have ... If he had asked me in the evening when I was knackered I might have refused' (Shute, 2016; Telegraph, online). Toby was barely literate and not practised in letter writing. However, over two subsequent years, with the help of his mum finding contacts for him via Facebook, he had written 681 letters including to all 193 United Nation member states. Toby now has his own book with some of his favourite letters entitled *Dear World, How are you?* This illustration is certainly not typical, yet it illustrates what a little imaging can do. The extent to which the process of feedback can become part of a child's imaging and part of looking forward with curiosity into a learning future seems worth some exploration.

## Attempts to conceptualise curiosity

There is a large and increasing volume of literature on curiosity that is particularly located within cognitive psychology. (Berlyne (1954) and Loewenstein (1994) both offer a comprehensive review and chronology.) This chapter spotlights literature that may enhance our appreciation of the bearing of curiosity within the classroom context of English education. Accordingly, our grasp of policy and practice may be strengthened by exploring theoretical grounds for locating curiosity in current educational concerns.

Dewey's distinction between types of curiosity is a helpful starting point. Dewey (1910) distinguished three types of curiosity. Firstly, physical curiosity. 'In its first manifestations, curiosity is a vital overflow, an expression of an abundant organic energy. A physiological uneasiness leads a child to be "into everything," – to be reaching, poking, pounding, prying' (31). This seems to be associated by Dewey with early life experiences, when the child is very young. A second type of curiosity accompanies this, which he identifies as social curiosity.

> [A] higher stage of curiosity develops under the influence of social stimuli. When the child learns that he can appeal to others to eke out his store of experiences, so that, if objects fail to respond interestingly to his experiments, he may call upon persons to provide interesting material, a new epoch sets in. 'What is that?' 'Why?' become the unfailing signs of a child's presence ... the search is not for a law or principle, but only for a bigger fact.
>
> *(Dewey, 1910: 32)*

As the child gains more knowledge, there becomes a greater need to make sense of it, to derive laws and principles. It is at this point, he suggests his third type of curiosity, which becomes intellectual 'rising above curiosity' that is physical or social.

> It is transformed into interest in problems provoked by the observation of things and the accumulation of material. When the question is not discharged by being asked of another, when the child continues to entertain it in his own mind and to be alert for whatever will help answer it, curiosity has become a positive intellectual force.
>
> *(33)*

Within the English school system Dewey's first two notions of curiosity are well embedded into both policy and practice in the Early Years and Foundation Stage (EYFS) (DfE, 2012b). It could be argued that the change in emphasis as the children progress through the EYFS (aged 3–5) into year 1 (aged 5–6) could be in line with a shift to Dewey's third type of curiosity. This would certainly provide some underpinning for the changing emphasis in the curriculum documents across the early years (ages 3–5) and KS1 (aged 5–7) age phases. In promoting intellectual curiosity, Dewey suggests that its drivers are quite different. 'Physical' and 'social' curiosity seem to be driven by the child, and rewarded by the world around and interactions with it. There seems to be a different driving force for intellectual curiosity. So much so that 'if germinating powers are not used and cultivated at the right moment, they tend to be transitory, to die out, or to wane in intensity' (33). He also suggests that the subject focus for intellectual curiosity becomes increasingly narrow and focused as the child gets older.

If Dewey's key points, about the drives and focus for curiosity changing, are to be heeded, the teacher needs to know how to help utilise and direct pupils' curiosity. Clearly, there is recognition that children do not present themselves as universally curious, thus the context of their learning and the impact of teaching needs greater understanding. If curiosity changes, the question needs to be raised as to whether curiosity is a 'state' or a 'trait'. That is, are there differences amongst individuals that are fixed or are they changeable (e.g. Naylor, 1981)? If curiosity were identified as a trait it would be considered to be fairly fixed in an individual across all situations. Although Kashdan et al. (2004) state that even if there is a trait-like feature there may be malleability (292). Whereas, if it were a 'state' it would vary in different situations. Discussions in the literature that fracture curiosity in this simplistic 'either/or' manner may not be helpful in understanding how best to nurture and foster children's curiosity in the classroom. It immediately raises an issue that for children who are not curious (or not sufficiently curious) there is some sort of deficit within them which cannot be easily changed. Day (1982: 21) indicates that there are likely to be elements of both state and trait influences and it is the understanding of both that is of importance, particularly in the classroom. Further attention is given in the next section to understanding curiosity in terms of how it might be formed and sustained.

## What drives curiosity?

Dewey's ideas seem to resonate with others who have subsequently looked at curiosity. Certainly the developmental psychology of Piaget and Vygotsky draws upon notions of curiosity as driving forces in children's learning. If curiosity forms part of this learning process, then it seems vital that some grasp of it is drawn into our understanding of the mechanisms that are designed to enhance learning – such as feedback. Furthermore, if curiosity is also part of the regulatory process that influences learning, then there is further weight to its importance.

Berlyne's work in the 1950s made a distinction between 'perceptual' curiosity and 'epistemic' curiosity (1954). Berlyne refined Dewey's notion and has been a foundation for subsequent thinking on curiosity. *Perceptual curiosity* relates to a stimulus having a property such as being novel or unusual that attracts attention whereas *epistemic curiosity* describes a human behaviour, a desire for knowledge. Berlyne considered 'certain pieces of knowledge to be more ardently sought and more readily retained than others' (180). Berlyne's work leaves unanswered the question of what type of knowledge promotes perceptual curiosity and whether something can be 'done' to the knowledge so that an individual may become more curious to possess it. Neither does it give much insight into curiosity, in the epistemic sense, in which it is a human behaviour and desire. In a classroom context both are important. One is more linked to the teacher and his/her transformation of curriculum context into something that might evoke perceptual curiosity. The other is more firmly footed with the child, and his or her response to wanting to learn. The feedback process can therefore be a space where both are explored, recognising the curriculum context as well as the individual response – past, present and future.

Kashdan et al. (2004) claim that individual differences, interests, expectations and prior knowledge will all affect curiosity (292). Such insight renders it vital to ensure that individual differences are encapsulated within the feedback process. It also gives weight, not only to the inclusion of curiosity in the process of feedback, but to the importance of personalising the process. This necessarily frames it as an active personal process, which is not only a part of learning, but a part of living.

Day (1982), drawing on Berlyne's work, indicates that curiosity is a 'state of excitement and directed interest' (19). The 'tension', that excitement derived from uncertainty, induces results in explorative behaviour which becomes the basis for learning, and brings its own rewards. Day centres his view on an epistemic dimension to curiosity and on a neurophysiological model of arousal claiming (along with Berlyne) that an increase in arousal is sought because the resulting exploratory behaviour, which reduces the tension created, is rewarding and pleasurable. However, he suggests that there are limits. He advocates that there is a 'zone of curiosity', which lies between a 'zone of relaxation' and a 'zone of anxiety' (20). Maintaining this 'zone of curiosity' needs to be the focus for the teacher, and requires an understanding of the unique dispositions of individual pupils, and the way that the learning environment can be adapted to optimise learning.

Sustaining curiosity, suggests Loewenstein (1994), requires the recognition that the level of curiosity demonstrated relates to the gap between what is known and what someone desires to know. Loewenstein claims that a person's desire to fill his/her knowledge gap drives curiosity. What becomes crucial in this model is whether or not the size of the knowledge gap is seen as manageable by the individual. If it is too large or the processes of gaining that knowledge seem too daunting then the result may be that new knowledge is not sought. He suggests that a *feeling-of-knowing* (FOK) is important – a belief that you can achieve your goal. Loewenstein suggests that a lack of knowledge (a deprived state of knowledge) drives curiosity, rather than curiosity being the driver for more knowledge. The distinction may at first seem subtle. However, the difference is significant in understanding the role of curiosity in learning. It shifts us away from some of the earlier notions that curiosity is an innate drive, and it is curiosity itself that drives seeking new knowledge. It suggests instead, that curiosity is identified and promoted through the recognition by the learner of a knowledge gap.

This clearly links to the notion of the 'Zone of Proximal Development' discussed in the previous chapter. Here, the ZPD was less clearly linked to the learner's cognitive awareness, and more linked to a more knowledgeable other person present to introduce and engage with the learner in areas of learning that lie just beyond current development related to where 'new buds' of development are just emerging but are not yet matured. Loewenstein claims that as the FOK becomes stronger, then the individual will perceive the knowledge gap to be smaller or more attainable – this he claims intensifies curiosity. However, this model is ultimately based on some sense of emotional response to the FOK – whether in terms of a pleasant or adverse response to the perception of the knowledge gap. This notion sits comfortably alongside Day's 'zone of curiosity' and the importance of remaining in this zone or the emotional response would not be conducive for the individual to learn.

Speilberger and Starr (1994) offer a little more clarity on distinguishing between those who have high levels of trait anxiety who typically seemed to be less curious (linked with an experiment related to asking and answering questions). This high-lighted the suggestion that feelings of emotions may vary and are linked to levels of curiosity. Thus, the extent to which a positive emotional state is achieved, derived from the sense of the need to alter a learning gap, seems to be the driver for curiosity. Thus Day (1982), Loewenstein (1994) and Speilberger and Starr (1994) recognise a relationship between curiosity and emotional states. However, they fail to resolve the tension between the two key modes of the promotion of curiosity. One concerns the reduction of a learning gap, designated as a sense of deprivation. The other involves the search for the satisfaction from something interesting. Litman (2005) pursues this distinction and suggests that perhaps both of these notions need to be embraced (799). Underpinning characteristics for curiosity, Litman (2005) claims, are related to both 'wanting', perhaps because of deprivation or perhaps because of the possibility of gaining rewards, and 'liking', a more complex set of feelings of interest. The juxtaposition of 'wanting' and 'liking', he claims, gives rise to the various ways in which individuals exhibit curiosity.

## Curiosity in the classroom context of pupil feedback for learning

This chapter has sought to tease out an individualist perspective and the extent to which this may or may not be important within conceptualising feedback for learning. The importance of the notion of curiosity is embedded within the policy context of education in England, and incorporated into one of the Teaching Standards for all teachers. Yet, such a notion seems to be located in a perspective of curiosity that assumes that teachers are able to promote intellectual curiosity in a similar sense to Berlyne's identification of 'perceptual curiosity'.

Schmitt and Lahroodi (2008) are so bold as to consider

> curiosity to be instrumental to and even essential for education, inquiry, and knowledge [and] is confirmed by the fact that teachers often prefer techniques of instruction that excite curiosity – they juxtapose topics with unexpected connections to elicit surprise, ask students questions to solve puzzles, present vivid examples or make striking demonstrations to rivet attention on the subject matter.
>
> *(125)*

Even though Schmitt and Lahroodi present a clear relationship between how teachers teach by stimulating curiosity, their contribution is still potentially limiting. There is no exploration of the interface between teaching for curiosity (which is what seems to be promoted) and learning. There seems to be a pervading possibility, building on Dewey's insights, that a failure to cultivate intellectual curiosity may leave it waning. But how much of such a possible fate should be laid at a teacher's feet? Epistemic notions of curiosity (Berlyne, 1954; Day, 1982; Loewenstein, 1994) locate a drive for curiosity that is identified through the perception of the knowledge gap (Loewenstein, 1994) or curiosity zone (Day 1982) and the emotions associated with the closing of the gap or remaining in the zone (Lit. 2005).

Drawing on Day (1982), Litman (2005), Loewenstein (1994), and Speilberg and Starr (1994) there is a complex interplay of knowledge and feelings of knowing (FOK) that will uniquely influence the extent to which any child might engage with learning. Accordingly, although not dismissing some of the teaching ideas that Schmitt and Lahroodi (2008) suggest, there is a level of focus needed which lies beyond teaching techniques or curriculum content which seem to have the learning gap as its heart.

In exposing another way of conceptualising the importance of the learning gap, there is a new and important dimension to feedback. The idea that there is a 'curiosity gap', which is part of the 'space' in which next steps of learning are taken, adds an important dimension to our understanding of the form and function of feedback. It recognises that learning is a specific personal process, even if the outcomes being sought give little recognition of this. Building on the relational perspective discussed in the previous chapter, it brings to the forefront that the process of feedback is for both the teacher and the pupil. Both need to learn from the process and the voice of each should be recognised.

Recognising that pupils have an emotional stake in the lived experience of their education is complex and not easy to define or measure. It points to both the uncertainty of learning outcomes, and the uncertainty of learning processes. In Biesta's terms it captures 'the beautiful risk of education' (Biesta, 2013). In Giroux's (1997) terms recognising the 'language of possibility' is all important (140). What Giroux promotes is the importance of a creative interplay of teacher and pupil voices to facilitate and appreciate the dominant culture of a prescribed curriculum which also recognises lived experience. For a child's intellectual curiosity to be supported, and for there to be a sharing of lived experience of learning, student voice cannot merely be reduced to the immediacy of performance (Giroux, 1997: 124). This has more recently been promoted by Craft and Chappell (2016) who highlight the importance of shaping the curriculum in a way that points to 'what if'. This encapsulates the essence of curiosity, and the role of feedback, which can be a communicative mechanism to restate and re-direct this essential question.

Accordingly, it is incumbent upon the class teacher to appropriate the curriculum so as to sustain and understand the child's curiosity making sense of curriculum opportunities which will boost progress. This will require more than the reproduction and conveyance of a prescribed curriculum in the classroom. Without such attempts it could be argued that not only might a child's curiosity wane (Dewey, 1910) but that 'distorted' communications, founded on the basis of schooling being about reproducing dominant cultures, may result in diminished learning. The argument here is not intended to be a polarisation of a dominant discourse of a prescribed curriculum against a critical pedagogy of resistance, permitting pupils to pursue an aimless diet of whatsoever they please. Indeed, contemporary educational debate, in which there are polarisations of competing theoretical standpoints, often seem unproductive. Rather, the argument is intended to help teachers to understand how children's curiosity might be both understood and sustained in order to seek to conceive and create suitable classroom environments.

From the discussion presented, curiosity may be usefully regarded as being part of the learning gap between what is known and what an individual wants/needs to know. An individual's perception and feeling of this gap is of significant importance to whether or not learning will be attempted – that is, to alter the gap. The pupil's reason for engaging with what is identified here as the 'curiosity gap' may be a result of 'wanting' or ' liking' the feel of the new knowledge – Day (1982), Litman (2005), Loewenstein (1994), Speilberger and Starr (1994). Essential skills for the teacher concern helping children identify and manage their learning so that they are supported in learning encounters that successfully help them use curiosity as a driver for their learning. It requires the teacher to be able to identify when the curriculum leads to disinterest, curiosity or anxiety, and for which children. Strategies that may be useful in this endeavour may include feedback which helps pupils understand steps to move their learning forward (not to close the gap, but engage and shift it). It must therefore be bi-directional. Furthermore, it must help pupils recognise the ways in which their own self-efficacy and self-regulation will affect the extent to which they feel able to consider making steps in their own learning.

This chapter has explored another dimension of the learning gap which feedback seeks to alter. There is a different type of altering of the gap conceptualised here. There is an opening to a possible learning future, which influences the *feeling* of the learning gap to the pupil. Feedback in this context must include being sensitive to personal interest. Teachers must seek to balance learning within the zone of curiosity, steering clear of the boundaries of relaxation (disinterest) and anxiety. To some extent this chapter offers further underpinning for Torrance and Pryor's (1998) notion of divergent feedback. It frames feedback very differently from the deterministic (chapter 4) or relational approach (chapter 5).

# 7

## REVEALING PUPILS' LEARNING GAP IN NUMERACY AND LITERACY WITH PUPILS WHO STRUGGLE TO SUCCEED

## A case study

### Chapter overview

This chapter presents the views of some pupils who struggle to achieve in classrooms in England. The chapter seeks to present their understandings of learning and feedback in order to tease out their priorities and thoughts about their learning. The chapter is a deliberate attempt to present the ways in which pupils make sense of and enact the feedback they are offered. It particularly seeks to make sense of the way in which pupils construct and control their own learning gap. Furthermore, it highlights how many of the pupils have not aligned their thinking in the ways that their teachers have expected. This highlights a range of insights about feedback, and challenges existing assumptions which require further attention.

### The context of classroom feedback

A significant part of the argument presented so far in this book recognises that feedback is about connecting the learning gap from now to next. The ways in which this needs to be understood are far more complex than the way it is most frequently enacted in classrooms or discussed in research. In a school context, feedback is typically framed by teachers clearly stating what should be learnt next. Pupils are invited to respond, correct and even comment as part of their response to feedback they receive. As discussed in chapter 4, the school system in England gives a structured curriculum and expectations of pupil achievement, which are tested at particular stages of learning. In an international arena in which standards in England seem to be failing compared to other jurisdictions, there is a deliberate attempt in national policy to raise standards. This has resulted in learning becoming more prescriptive in areas in which national testing has becomes high stakes. The requirement for pupils to demonstrate their learning in mathematics and English through national tests has resulted in the curriculum in these areas being distorted, prioritising that which is tested in order to facilitate gaining the best test scores. Feedback has become hijacked by this discourse, resulting in it being increasingly tight, more precise and focused on particular learning outcomes (Clarke, 2000; Murtagh, 2014). As argued in chapter 4, pupils' learning gaps (as determined by teachers) become far more predetermined, and the adjustments required for learning to progress become more tightly focused, prescribed and controlled.

The other ways in which feedback needs to be understood, as relational and individualistic (chapters 5 and 6), seem to be given little overt consideration in classrooms. Although much of this book is a conceptual re-exploration of feedback, serious attention is given to making sense of the classroom context and the pupils' experiences. The case study data used in this chapter is not intended to offer generalisable evidence of pupils' understanding and responses to feedback. It is used to illustrate how some pupils, for whom current school experiences do not enable them to reach expected achievement, make sense of their learning and feedback.

Articulating approaches to feedback is increasingly an essential part of policy at all school phases. Clear school-based policy decisions outline how feedback should be given, and often there are particular practices that are intended to unify approaches throughout schools or key stages. There are often particular ways of working that push feedback into formulaic practices. These are often carried out as part of a visible evidence trail aimed at showing how teachers have made a difference and engaged with learning, rather than about linking with student thinking. The widespread nature of these more 'visible' practices promoted a response by the inspection agency in England, when Ofsted published a statement about the myths of feedback, in order to reduce these formulaic practices.

> Ofsted recognises that marking and feedback to pupils, both written and oral, are important aspects of assessment. However, Ofsted does not expect to see any specific frequency, type or volume of marking and feedback; these are for the school to decide through its assessment policy. Marking and feedback should be consistent with that policy, which may cater for different subjects and different age groups of pupils in different ways, in order to be effective and efficient in promoting learning.
>
> *(Ofsted, 2016, section 5)*

Apparent nationally in England was that feedback had to be considered more carefully in terms of what it was achieving, rather than just being visible for no clear purpose other than providing evidence for inspectors. Whole school policies in which feedback practices were standardised across different key stages raise a whole new set of issues in relation to the skills, abilities and development milestones of the children who receive them. Part of my own motivation for looking more deeply into feedback stems from my experiences visiting classrooms in which books were beautifully marked, with feedback written in different coloured pens, but some children were unable to read it or act on it.

In addition to very mixed responses to feedback in terms of learners' technical engagement, there seems to be contradictory evidence about its impact. For some learners, no matter how tight the feedback focus becomes or how frequently it is given, whether it is written in their books, stuck on their desks or dangled over their heads (all strategies featuring in classrooms), there are some pupils who struggle to make sense of it in a way that results in improved learning.

The purpose of this chapter is therefore to explore in a little more depth the ways in which pupils make sense of their learning and particularly the feedback and next steps which are designed to steer it in particular ways. It gives the opportunity to test out some of the theoretical possibilities which previous chapters have addressed. In particular, the way in which pupils understand and construct their learning gap can be more closely considered. The chapter also reveals the ways in which pupils use and interpret the feedback they are given. Of significance, is how pupils are positioned within teaching and learning so that their perspectives on feedback can be explored. This chapter draws on small-scale research, part of which I have previously published (Dann, 2015). However, this chapter extends the considerations and widens the research to include further data and analysis.

## Pupil identity and learning

Notions of identity are certainly not new. Often they have been associated with terms such as character, traits or personality. There is certainly some sense in which learning requires purpose and intention. This is evident at a national policy level as well as in classrooms where lesson intentions and outcomes are made explicit. Particular assumptions are often made about the ways in which pupils will respond to the learning opportunities in which they are placed. As the research about feedback reveals, we must begin to explore why some individuals respond differently to the same taught experiences. If feedback is more precise and more focused on learning outcomes, why is it not always effective to the same extent? Vygotsky grappled with the same question. The discussion offered in chapter 5 highlights pupil learning within a constructivist model. It recognised that all participants differently understand learning contexts, and that there is a relational aspect to the way in which learning (and development) advances. Such considerations give agency to pupils to make sense of their own learning.

Discussions in chapters 4, 5 and 6 offer very different ways in which a child's learning gap (gap between learning now and next), which feedback seeks to alter, might be constructed, controlled and changed. The argument, which builds in this book, is centred on how and if pupils 'fit into' theoretical, practical and policy formations of a learning gap. Each of the conceptualisations of the learning gap outlined has a legitimate claim on understanding and framing the notion of a learning gap. However, there is a clear and emphatic articulation throughout previous chapters that the pupil (as learner) must be central to issues about learning and mediates any shift in their own learning gap. Their own 'lifeworlds' (Habermas, 1984) are interwoven with their learning of school knowledge. Although

understanding the learning gap between now and next is important in the relational process of teaching and learning, schools need to do more. Moll (2010)
suggests that 'when students witness the validation of their culture and language,
hence of themselves, within the educational process, when they "see themselves"
in their schooling, they combine their home or community identities with an
academic identity' (456).

As children progress through compulsory schooling, their engagement is not
only about learning (yielding particular outcomes) but also about their evolving
learner (academic) identity. The learning gap, which might be constructed in very
particular ways around notions of now and next, is therefore intricately bound up
with relationship (or gaps) between an individual and his/her identity within different contexts and cultures. The extent to which individuals see themselves as
learners will certainly influence the way in which they chose to engage with the
opportunities afforded to them. Having any identity, Gee (2000–2001) claims,
requires some interpretative system which helps make sense of 'self' in context. As
children are in the process of shaping their learner identities, feedback can be seen
as a mediating tool, which offers specific information and direction for particular
learning outcomes. However, it also contributes to (and sits alongside) the way
individuals form multiple identities (e.g. pupil, daughter, friend, male, living in a
flat, being in blue group, being in scouts, achieving a task, having some correc-
tions…) and self-author themselves into specific cultural and social contexts. Holland et al.'s (1998) notion of 'Figured World' (FW) provides a useful framework
for locating this chapter into the wider discourse of learner identity.

Holland et al. (1998) seek to locate their theory of FW beyond both the culturalist
and constructivist approaches, which they identify as 'opposing' (10). They interpret
the culturalist position as how an individual is positioned within major structural
features of society (e.g. ethnicity, gender, race, nationality, p. 7). The constructivist
view they summarise as social positioning which happens within social interactions
(11). Holland et al., however, offer a different view, in that people (individually
and collectively) are not simply a product of a cultural or social situation, but are
'critically appropriators of cultural artefacts that we and others produce' (17). In a
school context this locates pupils as active agents in their constructions of self. Holland
et al. also make clear that self is not considered as a singular identity but as plural. There
are multiple and sometimes competing sites of self-production (29) and that self is seen
as always in practice or in production rather than static or in essence. They present the
notion of 'self-in-practice' as a process of 'self-authoring'. This draws on Bakhtin's
views (in Holland et al.) which promote the importance of speech and language as the
means through which an individual self-authors. Each individual is continually and
actively in a process of either being 'addressed' or 'answering'. Thus, identities are
continually shifting, as the many voices of those around are 'orchestrated'.

Part of the way in which each person is seen as being many selves, is connected
to their being part of different figured worlds. Each FW offers different voices and
positioning to which an individual is addressed and answers. Holland et al., therefore,
identify a figured world as a

socially and culturally constructed realm of interpretation in which particular characters and actors are recognized, significance is assigned to certain acts, and particular outcomes are valued over others. Each is a simplified world populated by a set of agents …who engage in a limited range of meaningful acts or changes of state … as moved by a specific set of forces.

*(52)*

For pupils in school, the particular figured world is their school and their particular positioning is their immediate school environment of the classroom. In aligning with Holland et al.'s thinking, this case study seeks to allow pupils to talk about their experiences of being in school. It tries to distil what they consider important, the messages that they hear, the 'significant others' they value and the perspectives they seek to answer and position themselves alongside. It recognises that a figured world is 'an abstraction, an extraction carried out under guidance' (53). From a school and teacher perspective (using Holland et al.) feedback is intended as a message system, culturally created and legitimated by teachers for conveying particular messages to pupils about their work and achievement. It is one of many cultural artefacts through which pupils will interpret their own understandings and positioning, in order to make sense of their developing selves in practice. The approach facilitates possible interpretations that seek understandings in many ways. It gives agency to all participants and recognises that meaning cannot be pre-assumed.

## Case study data

The focus of the research study undertaken here is to work with a small number of children across three schools. The children selected are aged 9–10 who struggle to achieve at the nationally determined 'expected' level in numeracy and literacy but do not have a specially identified special need. Although there are some interesting findings that will be discussed, the chapter also seeks to tease out a process for pupil engagement which helps to shift the emphasis away from particular feedback techniques to broader approaches for situating feedback and learning in broader discussions about pupils' learning, lives and personal identities. The research focuses on how pupils make sense of themselves as learners, and the place that feedback has in this process.

Initially, 22 pupils were involved in the study through one-to-one interactions with the researcher across two schools. There were 12 children (aged 5–6) in year 1 (six in each school) and 10 pupils (aged 9–10) in year 5 (five in each school: six boys and four girls). The year 1 pupil sessions continued for only three sessions per pupil in this study and this data was used for contextual and comparative purposes and for considering the most appropriate age for the start of future work. (It is not specially reported here.) A further school was involved 18 months later with four new children (aged 9–10, two boys, two girls) being involved in a similar sequence of five one-to-one sessions. All three schools were categorised as being in an areas of high social deprivation with free school meal numbers of over 40 per cent. Each school was within a different Local Authority.

## Focus and structure

The five sessions were designed to explore the children's understanding of their own learning and particularly how they understood what learning was needed next from their own perspective and their views of their teacher's perspectives. Their use and understanding of feedback and targets was also explored.

Sessions were structured with the following priorities (only selections from the research are included in this chapter):

- Enabling pupils to talk about their experiences of learning (session 1).
- Try to establish what they considered to be their next steps in learning in numeracy and literacy (sessions 2 and 4★).
- Tease out their own priorities for learning, and discuss and compare these with their perceptions of their teacher's priorities (sessions 2 and 4★).
- Invite the children to articulate their own future targets/next steps (sessions 2 and 4★).
- Give opportunities for the pupils to develop targets and to use and construct feedback (session 3★).
- Explore what they thought being at school offered them in relation to their own aspirations (sessions 1, 2 and 4★).
- Explore if and how they could take on the views of another (multiple perspectives) when there were issues of tension and conflict (session 5★★).
- Try out how they could develop arguments for their decisions about their own learning and the learning choices they make in a task (session 5★★).

(★The order of sessions was altered with the last school so that session 4 was undertaken as session 3 and session 3 became session 4.)

(★★Session 5 was adjusted in the final school so that it focused on pupils justifying their own learning priorities, identifying success criteria, reviewing their own work and seeking to establish how they were building on the feedback they had previously received.)

## The challenge of learning

Twelve of the 14 children (aged 9-10) were positive about their school experiences. However when asked whether learning was 'hard' or 'easy' each seemed to indicate that there were elements of challenge as well as aspects which were 'quite' hard. Each seemed to identify something that they felt that they could do, but they also indicated areas of struggle. There seemed to be some tension for them in being sure of what was difficult, why, and how they were approaching such struggles. Very different issues were highlighted by the children. There was no consistency in the data over what these are or how they might be resolved. Three are offered below by way of illustrating that there are significant struggles, which if understood better might give some insight into how learning could become more successful.

## *What's hard and what's easy? (Transcript extract 1)* *(also partially cited in Dann, 2015: 11)*

(FEMALE) S1:2:  Maths is like a bit hard and like a challenge to me. Literacy is really easy.

R:  …what else is hard?

S1:2:  Nothing. [Silence]

R:  It is just the maths … How does your teacher help you?

S1:2:  Sometimes. She is helpful, but sometimes I am scared to put up my hand in case she says 'No'.

R:  You are worried to put your hand up? So what do you do instead?

S1:2:  We have cards like red … green and you put them out.

R:  So do you put yours on to red if you are stuck?

S1:2:  No.

R:  So even if you are stuck you do not turn your red one over?

S1:2:  No.

R:  So are you worried that she will not help you?

S1:2:  Yes.

R:  Do you think she would mind, or does she think you are not trying hard enough … [Pause and a shrug] … You're not sure? OK, so perhaps you will have to be a bit braver. …

In this instance it is clear that the communication (feedback) system initiated by the teacher to enable learning difficulties to be identified within lessons, so that teaching and learning could be more successful, was not being interpreted by the pupil in the way intended. This narrative raises a range of important issues. Firstly, and of greatest interest, is the problematic relationship that the pupil identifies in her learning context. For some reason, this pupil has a level of fear that prevents her from using the feedback processes established in the classroom in her mathematics lessons. (This was not the case in literacy.) It would appear that she was not comfortable indicating to the teacher that she did not understand aspects of her mathematics. She would prefer to struggle than to ask. This conversation also reveals that a dialogic encounter, such as the one developed as part of this research, may not have yielded the same responses if the pupil had been conversing directly with her teacher. It demonstrates that, in this case, the pupil retreats from channels through which she can gain help, although the reasons for this are not clear. It also reveals that for this pupil she adopts a very different response to the challenge of learning between mathematics and literacy. She uses feedback, and the support from the teacher, in very different ways. These seem to be associated with her confidence in the subject area, rather than the strategies the teacher adopts. She very clearly identifies mathematics as a subject she does not like and finds difficult. The only target (or future learning) in mathematics she could identify for her own progress was to improve her times tables. She was not able to indicate what her teacher was hoping she would learn next. This pupil was clearly trying to shut down her learning gap in mathematics, perhaps to reduce the level of challenge which she clearly encountered.

One of the difficulties with the pace of the National Curriculum, and the pressure of pupils being required to achieve expected (or greater) achievements, is that the curriculum hurries on unabated. For children who struggle to succeed, very quickly they can be left behind. If pupils perceive the cognitive challenge to be too great, they will act in some way to reduce it (Butler and Winne, 1995; Kluger and DeNisi, 1996; Shute, 2008). For this pupil, she has clearly indicated that classroom communication systems used to help the teacher understand difficulties in lessons, are to be avoided. The coloured card system is a cultural artefact designed to convey particular messages. However, it is clear that she has disassociated herself from it and instead has used it to convey that she has no problems. This may be an attempt to cushion her feelings associated with finding mathematics hard. Furthermore, it provides her with an opportunity to signal to the teacher that she is being successful in the lesson, when in fact she is not.

An extract from another transcript indicates how a pupil struggles to make sense of the challenge that the curriculum offers. To some extent, the comment below shows that the pupil does not have a fixed notion of whether he can tackle the curriculum or not. He is flexible in taking on a challenge. However, there is a fundamental drawback for this pupil when he is required to be more imaginative.

### What's hard and what's easy? (Transcript extract 2) (also cited in Dann, 2015: 11)

(MALE) R.: What is really easy?
(MALE) S2:1: Maths. The others are mainly easy [pause] mainly hard.
R: What is hard?
S2:1: Literacy. Science is a bit hard.
R: What makes literacy hard?
S2:1: Too much writing.
R: Is it the actual picking up the pen and writing that is the problem?
S1: No, the thinking. I can't think of the stuff to write.

Transcript 3 reveals a similar difficulty. The pupil wants to understand his learning in terms of right and wrong. Literacy does not seem to fit into this mould. His levels of uncertainty as to whether or not it is correct, or whether he has not clearly understood what is acceptable, creates a problem. This is important information for a teacher. It clearly signals particular needs that the learner has for understanding his work. Also, it identifies possible areas for misalignment with the teacher's requirements and expectations.

### What's hard and what's easy (Transcript extract 3)

(MALE) S3:1: I like maths better than English because you have to think for the answers you want.

R: You nearly always get an answer in maths…

S3:1: Yeh, like poems where there's no right or wrong answer. In acrostic poems and you get told to rhyme. I don't know how they are supposed to rhyme in acrostic poems …

R: Do you find it hard sometimes to get your ideas down on paper?

S3:1: Yeah cos the other thing I like about maths is that if you get it wrong you can cross it out and then you know you've made a mistake.

R: Can't you do that in English?

S3:1: No, not much. Cos in English you are told to write your own story. There's no right or wrong answer.

R: So sometimes in English you are not sure if it's the right or wrong thing?

S3:1: No, the only thing you can get wrong in English is your punctuation and spellings.

Each of the pupils in the study showed clear engagement with their school and classroom environment. They had understood that they were learners, but clearly showed preferences for how they understood and engaged with their learning. They knew that learning is not a problem-free experience and chose to experience and act on elements of it differently. Their own learner identities were not straightforward for them to grasp and understand, but they had clear elements of preference, difficulty, struggle and uncertainty.

## A purpose for school learning

In the first session with the children they had been asked why they thought they came to school and what it might offer them. Also, if they had any idea of what they wanted to do when they were older, and whether school would help to achieve this. This was part of an attempt to see how they understood learning and school as part of their own life development. It was clear that all children in all three schools enjoyed being at school and in some sense saw themselves as learners, wanting to learn. However, these 14 pupils had very different notions of why they were at school and what they thought they might benefit from their experience. To illustrate, extracts from all four pupils from school three are used to highlight their thinking about what school and learning are for.

## What is the purpose of school and learning? (Transcript extract 4)

R: Why do you think you have to come to school?

S3:1: So we can learn about education and if we went straight to high school we wouldn't have any idea what to do. So they would have to teach us from the start.

R: So you come to primary school to get ready for high school? (Child agrees.)

S3:1: You start in reception because you don't know that much so they teach you more things in reception and when you get into the higher classes they teach you more and more.

R: Do you think the work gets harder as you get older?

S3:1: And when you get into year 5 they reteach you things you've already learnt, so they can refresh your mind.

R: What skills does school give you?

S3:1: They give you more skills than if you're home-schooled.

R: So what kind of skills – can you think?

S3:1: Long division, long multiplication and then I think this was in Y2, 3 or 4 … there was a different method for 'timesing' …

R: What skills do you think you get for English?

S3:1: They teach you about punctuation where they might not in home-school.

R: And any other skills you might learn in school?

S3:1: Embedded clauses.

R: What's an embedded clause?

S3:1: It's where you use two commas and it's extra information – it's like brackets and dashes. And then there's colons and semi-colons that you can use.

R: And do you enjoy learning about other punctuation? Do you find that interesting?

S3:1: Yes. Cos we relearn skills each day. From years 3 and 4.

R: So when you grow up what would you like to be?

S3:1: I don't really know yet.

R: Any ideas at all?

S3:1: No.

R: So when you've finished primary school, you'll then go to high school and then what do you think you'll do after high school?

S3:1: I might go to college so I can get a job and then when I've finished college – I'm not sure – but I might go to university.

R: What do you do at university?

S3:1: You learn more about your job I think, getting ready for the actual improvements in your job.

R: So would you like to do something with maths maybe?

S3:1: I might like to do something like my sister and work at the food place. Cos she works at McDonalds in [name of city …].

R: And will school help you?

S3:1: They will in maths because unlike English you're not going to write a 300 word essay to become a cashier.

R: I see but will school help you to get a job in the future?

S3:1: Yeah.

R: How?

S3:1: Cos it can teach you the right words to say because you've been writing so that can help you in the words you speak. And in Maths it's easier to use a cash machine cos you know what numbers to click, cos you know the prices and about money.

### What is the purpose of school and learning? (Transcript extract 5)

R: Why do we have to come to school?

S3:2: Because if we didn't come to school we wouldn't know much and we wouldn't succeed in life. Everyone would have to live on the streets because they wouldn't make money. If you work in a shop you have to know what to do and you have to know where to put the stuff. You need to be able to do your maths and stuff if you work on the tills.

R: So what skills does school give you then?

S3:2: It teaches us how to talk English properly, how to teach people and if you become a teacher in all sorts of schools and you can go to university and teach.

R: What skills do you think you're learning in school?

S3:2: The simple ones. The basic ones that come into everyday life like reading clocks. I'm not very good at that but I can still try. And if you are refurbishing something you need to know if you're putting laminate in ... you need to know how much you need ... to use metres to measure around so you know how much carpet you're putting in ...

R: So what would you like to be when you're older?

S3:2: I don't know ... I want to be a mechanic but my dad says I can't. I'd like to be a doctor.

R: What do you think you have to do to become a doctor?

S3:2: Go to university, go to the college ... study for years and years and years, for a long time. You have to pass the courses and things like that.

R: Will school help to do that?

S3:2: Schools help to do that. You won't in primary schools. You might learn a bit in high school and college but university will help the most ...

### What is the purpose of school and learning? (Transcript extract 6)

R: Why do you think you have to come to school?

S3:3: To learn, so when you become an adult you get money. You have a job and everything.

R: What skills does school give you? (hesitation) Or do you think school will help you to get a job? How?

S3:3: Yeah by learning me everything.

R: What kind of things?

S3:3: So if I be a scientist or something I can just remember when I was little and then I can just ... remember what I've done when I was little.

R: Would you like to be a scientist?

S3:3: Yeah

R: Is there anything else you would like to be when you grow up?

S3:3: I would like to be a dancer ...

R: What type of skills do you think school will help you with when you grow up? (Long delay from child) What will maths help you with when you're an adult? (no response)

R: OK ... What might it help you with in a shop?

S3:3: Getting change ...

R: What about writing? (No response) Do you think writing will help you as an adult or not?

S3:3: No

## What is the purpose of school and learning? (Transcript extract 7)

(From earlier discussion about targets and goals)

S3:4: I like my class because we get to learn and we get to achieve more stuff.

R: What does that word 'achieve' mean?

S3:4: It means like sometimes you want to reach your goals.

R: Have you got any goals you would like to reach?

S3:4: I want to be a nurse ...

R: Why do you think you have to come to school?

S3:4: Because if we stay at home all day we won't learn anything and when you're older you won't get like money for your family. When we're older we can get a job and get money for our family.

R: What skills do you think school gives you to do that?

S3:4: Determination.

R: What skills do you learn at school that will help you in the future?

S3:4: English, maths, writing. Challenge helps you in history...

R: Why do you want to be a nurse when you're older?

S3:4: Because you can help people and help them to live and you get a lot of money being a nurse.

R: How are you going to become a nurse, what will you have to do?

S3:4: You have to write, to be clever and then you have to be ready for the job.

R: And do you think school will help you to do that?

S3:4: Yeah.

The pupils clearly had a notion of school progression, identifying their own future journey through educational institution. Only transcript 6 did not include going to university or college. They thus had a broad sense of a gap from where they are now to where they want to be in the future when they leave secondary school – in terms of a physical educational learning space. Far more hazy in the minds of the pupils was the purpose of their current schooling. S3:3 had said that the learning needed for the future would not be done in primary school: 'You won't in primary schools'. However, S3:2, in his thinking around possibly being a scientist, thought that all his learning would be remembered from when he was little.

There was clearly some thinking around the usefulness of basic number skills, particularly in connection with shop work. They struggled to see the point of developing their writing (except for S3:4). S3:1 indicated 'you're not going to write a 300 word essay to become a cashier'. S3:4 was very clear that she saw no point in writing for her future. However, the value of speaking well was seen far more positively and was specifically mentioned by the pupils. All the pupils in this research study saw some value in their own future learning. They found it far more difficult to see themselves as learners, connecting their learning from past and present towards identified possible futures. Of course, this may not be completely surprising, being aged 9–10 their own developmental skills are not fully matured. More abstract thinking may remain a challenge. However, these pupils struggled to articulate clear reasons for why they were at school, and how school might help them. Their disposition was positive but vague. This finding has implications for the ways in which they engage and progress in their learning. Their understanding of their next steps for learning and engagement with their feedback and targets provide areas for further understanding their learning and progress.

## Learning 'next'

### Teacher and learner distinctions

Part of the research study involved asking the pupils to talk about their next steps of learning (in English and mathematics). The methods used are reported in more detail in Dann (2015). In essence, this was carried out in the one-to-one discussions over two separate sessions. The first of these sessions focused on English and the second on mathematics. The structure of both sessions was similar. In each session pupils were asked to say what they thought their next steps or targets were in one of the two subject areas. These were written down by the researcher on 'post-it' (sticky) notes (one target or next step on each note – using the same colour of post-its). When this was complete the pupils were asked if they could add any further targets or next steps which they thought their teacher had for them. These were written down on separate 'post-its' of a different colour.

Pupils were asked to order the sticky notes, putting the one that they thought was highest priority for them at the top, down to the least important at the bottom. When this task was complete, the rank order was noted on the corner of each post-it note. All the notes were then jumbled up. The pupil was then asked to pretend to be his/her teacher, and to put the targets (next steps) in the order of priority that s/he thought his/her teacher would hold. It was indicated that this could be the same or different from their ordering. The rank order was then noted in the opposite bottom corner. The purpose of this task was to try to understand how the pupils were shaping their learning gaps. Furthermore, it was intended to see how (and if) they were mediating between their own and their teacher's views (as perceived by the pupil) of next steps for learning.

In English, the pupils were able to identify a range of targets for themselves and ones which they thought the teachers had for them (see Dann, 2015). An example of the targets offered is given in Table 7.1

The data, included in Dann (2015), together with the data from an additional school, reveal a similar picture. Pupils were easily able to identify next steps and targets for learning in English. They offered priorities which they held for themselves and, when asked, provided additional targets or next steps that they thought

**TABLE 7.1** Learning targets for literacy (adapted from Dann, 2015: 14)

| Session 2 Literacy | Targets sequenced by the pupil in order of his/her priorities | Targets sequenced by the pupil in order of pupil-perceived teacher priorities |
| --- | --- | --- |
| S1:2 | 1. Speak what I want to write<br>2. Improve handwriting★<br>3. Listen to the teacher★ | 1. Listen to the teacher★<br>2. Improve handwriting★<br>3. Speak what I want to write |
| S1:3 | 1. Sometimes use the computer e.g. for school council questions<br>2. Using connectives★<br>3. Use of metaphors★<br>4. Check the size and spacing of letters★<br>5. Use a different colour pen | 1. Check the size and spacing of letters★<br>2. Using connectives★<br>3. Use of metaphors★<br>4. Sometimes use the computer e.g. for school council questions<br>5. Use a different colour pen |
| S2:2 | 1. Checking to make sure that your sentences make sense<br>2. Use of capital letters★<br>3. Use different types of sentences<br>4. Remember spellings with double letters★<br>5. Get better ideas★ | 1. Use different types of sentences<br>2. Checking to make sure that your sentences make sense<br>3. Use of capital letters★<br>4. Remember spellings with double letters★<br>5. Get better ideas★ |
| S2:3 | 1. Read it★<br>2. Finger spaces★<br>3. Cursive writing★<br>4. Capital letters and full stops★ | 1. Cursive writing★<br>2. Read it★<br>3. Capital letters and full stops★<br>4. Finger spaces★ |
| S2:4 | 1. Use more sentence types<br>2. Use more adjectives<br>3. Use more 2A [adjectives] sentences★<br>4. Some other sentences like 'more soldiers are brave, some are lazy'★<br>5. More DD sentences [descriptive detail]★<br>6. More rhetorical sentences★ | 1. Use more sentence types<br>2. Use more 2A [adjectives] sentences★<br>3. Use more adjectives<br>4. Some other sentences like 'more soldiers are brave, some are lazy'★<br>5. More DD sentences [descriptive detail]★<br>6. More rhetorical sentences★ |
| S3:1 | 1. Better presentation<br>2. Bit more work than you should do<br>3. Do more work than chatting★<br>4. More features in my work, like colons★<br>5. Smaller full stops★ | 1. Smaller full stops★<br>2. Do more work than chatting★<br>3. Better presentation<br>4. More features in my work, like colons★<br>5. Bit more work that you should do |
| S3:3 | 1. Use 'prove it' tasks to prove you can do it★<br>2. Improve my spellings<br>3. Improve use of my vocabulary – powerful words★<br>4. Be able to read trickier words<br>5. Describe characters' feelings and what they look like★<br>6. Use capital letters in the correct place | 1. Improve use of my vocabulary – powerful words★<br>2. Improve my spellings<br>3. Use capital letters in the correct place<br>4. Use 'prove it' tasks to prove you can do it★<br>5. Describe characters' feelings and what they look like★<br>6. Be able to read trickier words |

Perceived as teacher targets★

their teacher held for them. Only one pupil (S2:3) indicated that only teacher priorities were important and could not identify personal targets.

All of the pupils changed the order of ranking between their own priorities and those they thought were held by their teacher. In virtually all cases, a teacher target was placed first in the teacher ranking and a pupil target first in the pupil priority ranking. They clearly expressed a view that their priorities were different from their teacher's. They were happy to present this view and did not seem to have any problem with seeing their future learning in two different ways. It perhaps signals that they are clearly able to retain their own understandings and priorities in school, as well as to consider their teacher's views. They are thus able to elicit demarcations between their own and their teacher's priorities in English.

In mathematics there was a different picture. As reported by Dann (2015), the pupils in the two schools in the initial phase of the study struggled to offer next steps or targets in mathematics. There were a few suggestions related to needing to know their times tables better and being able to tackle harder sums. Virtually all of the pupils struggled to suggest any teacher priorities for 'next' steps in mathematics. The task of ordering and reordering was therefore not possible. Pupils in the third school offered a similar picture, although they did say a little more. Each of the four children in this school were able to identify targets for themselves and other targets from their teacher's perspective in mathematics. However, they were very unspecific and included targets such as 'challenge myself to do the next step', 'better presentation', 'stop speaking too much', 'work towards the next level and be on the table of champs'. There were a few mathematical targets such as 'improve my speed in mental maths', 'get higher scores in big maths', 'work on using division', 'using the big hand and little hand when telling the time'.

As reported in Dann (2015), it was particularly interesting that in two of the three schools pupils were not able to offer any or many targets or next steps in mathematics. They had little idea of what they needed to know next and could not indicate what they thought their teacher wanted them to know next. They clearly struggled to have any internal personal sense of next in mathematics. Interestingly, they did not follow the same strategy that was overwhelmingly used in literacy, which was to lower the level of their next steps to much easier ones. In the third school, pupils were more aware that progress was needed. The pupils certainly had a sense of there being higher levels for them to move onto, yet had little grasp of the mathematics to be achieved.

## Pupils' constructions of their own learning gap

In both these tasks, in English and mathematics, any subject-specific targets they were able to state were at a much lower level than the focus of current teaching. The next steps that the pupils had internalised were at a much more basic level. They included skills and knowledge about which they were already knowledge-able. They indicated areas in which they needed more practice or to be more consistent. Not only did they articulate their own targets in this way but they also identified their teacher's targets for them in these low level terms. This was despite the fact that success criteria for each lesson were stuck onto every page of their workbooks, and in two of the three schools pupil targets were stapled in the back covers of their workbooks.

The messages conveyed through teaching, marking and feedback had all been internalised differently by the pupils from the messages intended by their teachers. The reasons for this are not clear, and may include an attempt by pupils to make their personal learning challenges more manageable. They were therefore in some way reducing their cognitive load. Another possible interpretation is that the work was beyond their level of understanding, so that any attempts to improve needed to be altered by the pupils to be within a knowledge gap that they thought they could understand, and of which they could make sense. Another possible explanation, particularly in mathematics, relates to the mathematical content of teaching being insufficiently linked to pupil schema. Nutbrown (2011) offers some insight into the importance of linking schema (intrinsic forms and structures of thought) with content. The difficulty that the pupils had talking about their mathematics learning in any clear way seems to have some connection with their conceptual thinking being connected to what they were currently doing and might further develop.

Of course, part of the difficulties in developing notions and practice related to feedback with children is that they are still developmentally immature. Their skills in conceptualising, abstracting and thinking using high-order skills are less developed. Nevertheless, the process of learning requires there to be a sense of something beyond their current development. Also, it requires someone/something more knowledgeable, as well as having the intention and motivation to engage with both others and then oneself (see chapters 5 and 6). Even though their thinking may not yet be mature, they are learners. Given that these pupils were not making the progress that was expected in school, each was struggling to make sense of the messages that they were receiving about learning in the classroom. Although they were part of a classroom context in which teaching covered more advanced concepts and knowledge than they indicated, they were clearly 'orchestrating' a very different sense of themselves and their learning. What was very clear in this study was that the pupils had made sense of their prescribed learning environment and the tightly focused feedback messages in entirely their own way. It highlights pupils as active agents, constructing, deconstructing and reconstructing classroom messages. It also revealed that they had been offered few opportunities to present or discuss their own articulations of their learning priorities, and to overtly position their thinking alongside their teacher's before.

The children had a very limited sense of a learning gap in both subjects. They were more able to identify some parameters for what might be next in English than for mathematics. Yet in both areas, their sights were limited and their aspirations for learning minimal. The context of teaching and the specific predetermined feedback about their responses to it were not conveying the messages that were intended. What is revealed here is that no matter how tight and precise the feedback, it will not be heeded if it exceeds the recipient's interests, abilities or cognitive development, and is not alighted to their own learning priorities.

## Pupils' understanding of, and engagement with, written feedback

Part of the discussion with each pupil in the research study involved a focus on the written feedback their teacher had recorded on their work. Discussions were focused on recent work which included feedback comments, and particularly ones that the pupils chose. In this way it was hoped that the pupils would be able to choose the feedback that had the most meaning for them. Virtually every piece of written work had feedback comments designed to highlight what had been achieved (in green or pink ink) in relation to the success criteria as well as what needed to be improved. In one school yellow highlighting was used to indicate sentences for pupils to 'prove it' as a response. This was about checking for themselves whether they had done what was expected.

The children were clearly making some sense of their feedback. However, they were struggling to learn from it in the way their teachers intended. Three extracts are included here of the pupils talking about how they made sense of and used their teacher feedback. They have been selected to reflect three distinctive types of response that were evident from the pupil conversations. Firstly, the children were positive about having feedback and wanting to use it but were uncertain how to do this. This is exemplified in transcript 8. Secondly, they recognised that the feedback had a particular message but refused to act on it (transcript 9). Thirdly, they were unable/unwilling to accept the need for their work to change (transcript 10).

### *Understanding and using feedback (Transcript extract 8)*

(Looking at the latest piece of work – a letter)

R: It says: 'Look carefully at the sentence to see if you can improve it'.
    Do you know which sentence the teacher is talking about?
S3:1 (MALE): No, this is why I always look through it.
R: What do the yellow highlights mean?
S3:1: That's when we do 'prove it' and the teacher doesn't mark it – we do. We self-assess.
R: What do you think you have to do next to improve that sentence? (Reads for a while)
S3:1: I need to look through the sentences.
R: You're not quite sure how to improve that one?
S3:1: No
R: So this sentence that the teacher asked you to improve by reading it, have you been able to do that?
S3:1: No, I haven't seen which sentence it is or how to improve it.
R: So that's a bit tricky because you are not sure which sentence to improve.

In this feedback, the pupil is clearly not sure about what needs to be improved or why. Accordingly, he had not responded to the feedback. The feedback was insufficiently direct for the pupil to be able to consider it. However, even when a possible sentence for improvement was pointed out, he was not able to make any adjustments to the quality of his work in line with prompts to improve it. He was not able to see the limitations of his own writing or imagine that his writing could be different. There are much wider issues here than the focus of the specific teaching on grammatical structures. These link to the pupil having a notion of what learning might be 'next', and the sense of a small step which he can make to improve his work. The focus of the feedback here was well beyond his own construction of a learning gap. Accordingly, although recognising what the feedback was supposed to do to help improve, he had not been able to act on it.

### Understanding and using feedback (Transcript extract 9)

R: If you were looking at this piece of work, what would you do to improve it?
(FEMALE) S3:3: Er … mmmmm No, I think this writing's good.
R: Why are you happy with this piece of writing?
S3:3: Because I got green on the page.
R: So if the teacher writes something green – that means it's a good piece of work. What does the target say for this piece of work though?
(READ TOGETHER): 'Make sure you have a variety of reasons to call John home.'
R: What does that mean?
S3:3: To persuade him to come home.
R: Did you manage to do that, or was it difficult?
S3:3: It wasn't difficult, I just didn't do it.

In this example the feedback written in green pen conveyed the desired intention to the pupil. She is pleased that she has positive feedback. However, this has clearly overshadowed the 'development' comment. One of the main criteria for the piece of writing was to offer a letter of persuasion. In this example, the pupil did not think this was difficult but had chosen not to do it. Having looked at the pupil's work, it seems that this comment may well be a way of reducing the cognitive load of seeking to develop the type of writing required by the teacher. Rather than admitting that it might be a challenge, it was identified as something that she chose to ignore. This seemed to justify why the feedback had been ignored.

### Understanding and using feedback (Transcript extract 10)

R: Let's have a look at a recent piece of work. Now I have spotted this twice 'Uplevel your recount with a paragraph including inverted commas and commas for direct speech' …
(FEMALE) S3:4: Yeah.
R: So what do you have to do next time?

S3:4: He's saying that to use commas in a list and after openers.

R: What about inverted commas and commas? Do you understand what this means?

S3:4: I'm not sure.

R: So is this why your teacher has written it a couple of times?

S3:4: Yes.

R: Have you achieved that target now and can you use speech marks well in your work?

S3:4: I still need to work on it.

R: And if you were marking this piece of work, what would you do to improve it? Maybe something different from the teacher. (Child reads work.) Is there anything you would improve or are you happy with it?

S3:4: I'm happy with it.

R: What about other things you have been working on, like openers or fronted adverbials? Where could you include one? (Reads work and includes an opener.) Anything you could improve?

S3:4: No.

As well as recognising that she had not developed her skills in using commas or inverted commas, she also managed the demands made by the feedback by judging that she did not need to make further improvements. From the discussion, when questioned about recent work on sentence openers and fronted adverbials she declined to consider using any, instead stating the she did not think any further improvements were needed. She had very specifically disregarded information that she was not willing to act on, offering a justification for doing so.

## Seeing beyond yourself

The essence of the research outlined in this chapter focuses on the ways in which pupils see themselves as learners and use the information given to them through both feedback and targets as a way of progressing learning. It particularly focuses on pupils who struggle to succeed at the 'expected' nationally defined level. There are some fundamental issues that emerge from hearing the children talk about their classroom experiences, which help to frame the sense they make of their learning – past, present and future. The key issues are:

- Pupils mediate the messages that they receive from the feedback teachers give them about their next steps for learning.
- They repeatedly lower the level of challenge of the next steps for learning that are laid out for them by their teachers.
- They sometimes claim that they see no need for improvement, or to act on the feedback given.
- Sometimes they claim that they have chosen not to respond to the challenge presented in the feedback (although it seems in these cases this was to mask their lack of understanding of what they should do).

- They were able to give little indication of their next steps in learning.
- They were aware that their teachers had different priorities for their learning and confidently spoke of their own differing priorities in literacy.
- There was a difference between their understanding of their own learning gap in English and mathematics.
- Pupils demonstrated considerable agency in making sense of themselves as learners in school 'orchestrating' their own versions of the learners that they intend to be.

What seems clear from the glimpses that this study reveals is that pupils are not directed, controlled or regulated in the ways that teachers intend. Furthermore, they do not see their learning in such precise ways as the teacher shapes for them, or set themselves the challenges that the curriculum requires. It is recognised that these are children who have already demonstrated that they are not performing at the level expected. So they are not representative of pupils in general. Neither indeed are they necessarily representative of a particular defined grouping. What the study shows is that teachers are using feedback presumptively and assuming that the tightly defined targets, success criteria and feedback will be understood, interpreted and acted upon in particular ways. Quite clearly this is not always the case. The reasons for why this is not the case are more complex, and no exact causal reason is sought. The study reveals that pupils are more than willing to discuss what they think, and what their intentions are. They are also willing to discuss the views that they hold, and how these may differ from their teacher's.

It seems particularly important that if children are not achieving at the level expected there might be some dialogue with them that values their views, draws upon their thinking and their decisions about being a learner. The study revealed that in these schools this was not a feature of classroom practice in any genuine sense. The study exposes that the learning gap is visibly constructed and displayed by teachers within the curriculum in the classroom. Teachers acknowledge pupil differences, and seek to personalise feedback to particular errors and successes in each pupil's work. The feedback and targets set out clear steps intended to move the children's learning forwards to the expected levels. The dominant discourse, therefore, is related to predetermined standards regulated by teachers. The pupils in the study reveal a very different construction to their learning gap. They have personalised their school learning and synchronised the teachers' learning agenda with their own. In so doing, they significantly reduce, or even eliminate cognitive challenge. School learning is not a priority for them in the way that teachers intend, although they are engaged and willing to learn. It is also clear that in many cases their attempts to reduce their cognitive load may well be linked to their difficulties in conceptually matching the curriculum content to their own level of development and thinking schema, as well as not prioritising their learning in the way expected within the other strands of their lives.

The question that this study poses is, can there be better alignment of the ways in which next steps in learning are identified, shared and prioritised, between pupils and teachers? Furthermore, can a better understanding of the way in which the learning gap is conceptualised by different participants enable feedback (designed to alter the learning gap) to become a more useful mediating tool in the classroom? The following chapter begins to construct how such an approach might be conceptually framed using a more relational approach. It also offers some starting points for enactment.

# PART III

# New futures for feedback

# 8

# NEW WAYS FORWARDS IN CONCEPTUALLY SHAPING FEEDBACK FOR LEARNING

## Chapter overview

The scope of this chapter is to begin to outline how the pupil/teacher relationship can be realigned for productive pupil learning using feedback. In trying to conceptualise feedback differently, this chapter examines a number of significant considerations that aim to reshape how feedback may be constructed and enacted by both teachers and pupil in a situated relational communicative encounter. The first half of the chapter seeks to offer particular theoretical positioning that underpins more practical applications. These include establishing possibilities for pupil agency through exploring pupil power, positioning, and development within the feedback process. Key conceptual strands in this chapter look at the role of language and communication as essential components of education and through which feedback is understood and enacted. Issues of dialogue, democracy and deliberative communication are all explored. Additionally, Habermas' concept of communicative action (CA) is brought centre stage as a way of further identifying a possible framework for feedback.

The second half of the chapter looks at establishing principles that underpin the approach to feedback that is advanced in this book. A number of ideas and initiatives for development in practice are illuminated.

## Pupil agency

The arguments developed in chapters 5 and 6 in this book highlight the importance of both the relational encounter within feedback as well as the importance of understanding that final 'learning power' rests with the agency of individual learners to internalise what has been experienced so that it becomes part of their learning and subsequent development. Chapter 7 revealed some of the assumptions that are made by teachers about the way pupils interpret classroom instruction and guidance. This can result in teacher and pupil classroom priorities being misaligned. The tightening of teacher practices using focused objectives and clear success criteria can only partially impact on prompting pupil learning. If these articulations are not internalised by the pupils (or are interpreted differently) then teacher-constructed learning outcomes will not be demonstrated as expected or even desired. What has become clear in considering the process of feedback within the learning encounter is that teachers can only partially control and construct the impact of feedback. Whether formally acknowledged or not, pupils mediate the messages from teachers in their own ways and construct for themselves the 'learning gap' that they intend to be shaped. Whether this gap is similar to or overlaps that which is constructed by the teacher for learners is a crucial question. Certainly, teachers can influence this process, but it is less clear how it works and how different pupils choose to construct and control their learning gaps. As Perrenoud (1998: 87) indicates, feedback is not always accepted by pupils as teachers intend it to be. There are some insights, which require some further examination if feedback processes can be more fully understood as operating within a context in which pupils have agency as active participants.

What comes into play here is that pupils have agency over their developing self-regulatory processes as well as their mediating processes in a social world in which they position themselves against and alongside what 'others' say and do (Holland et al., 1998). How they choose to exercise such agency is far from straightforward to understand. This is certainly evident in the previous chapter, when children who do not meet expected progress talk about their own understandings and priorities for their learning.

Further research, with different distinctive cohorts of children, reveal quite different understandings. Keddie (2016) shows in her research with high-achieving 10–11 year-olds, that these children are able to internalise the neoliberal discourse that commodifies their learning outcomes. She found that children in her research were able to actively and purposefully mark out what would define them as highly achieving and try to ensure that they became and continued to be a 'good student'. This process was 'not without anxiety and inner conflict' (117). Each pupil in this study took on what Keddie framed as 'neoliberal responsibilisation' (116) in which they were self-determining and rational in the ways they responded to how the 'market' wanted them to be. They were acutely aware that their educational achievement was the key to their future success in life, and would help ensure that they were not doing menial jobs or living on the streets. There was also a strong link exposed in this study to the ways in which familial support helped to steer and reinforce the children's determination for success. The pupils recognised that the key determinant was their own hard work. However, this led to some of the pupils feeling under considerable stress as they repeatedly felt they had not achieved enough. They were developing their own strategies for 'playing the game' so that they could identify themselves as being more successful. These findings further support Wilkins' study (2012), but also point to some children being better at finding the advantages in 'playing' the neoliberal market, thus leaving other children, who are less savvy or not interested in playing this market, being more easily forced into identities of failure or under-achievement.

The agency of pupils to construct and shape their own learning identities is further and slightly differently considered by Scanlon (2016). In her study exploring 10-year-old boys as writers, she identifies how within the schooling system boys tend to be constructed as a 'problem' when their achievements in writing were considered. In her narrative study, the process of discussing with a small group of boys how they make sense of themselves as writers revealed that some of the assumptions that were made about boys as writers were unhelpful. Her research revealed that frequently used ideas to increase their engagement, such as developing 'boys' topics' within the curriculum, were based on assumptions that do not play out in her study. Rather, what the boys were demonstrating was that their writing was used to cement and affirm positive family times. They revisited themes and experiences that they associated with times of stability and enjoyment in their families, and it was these that offered motivation and engagement in their writing. Teachers, however, were seen to challenge or even refuse these pupil priorities in judging their work.

In both these research examples, pupils with certain privileges and dispositions were able to demonstrate particular understandings and interpretations of their own identities as learners. The ways in which these new understandings in these examples and the research outlined in the previous chapter have come into focus is through priority being given to pupils' narrativised accounts of their experiences. This allows insight into their learning to extend beyond the outcomes that might be tested or observed and reveal some of their thinking and feeling that they chose to articulate about their learning and experiences of school.

It seeks pupils' views in different ways, which are certainly adult directed, but are not teacher constrained and/or constructed. In a context of seeking to locate the pupil in the teacher/pupil relationship slightly differently than often seems to be the case in prevailing educational and classroom systems, there is an attempt here to re-establish pupil agency and position, and to bring this more centrally into understanding feedback for learning.

## Power and positioning

Of particular concern in understanding classroom feedback is how the power dynamics between pupil and teacher are regarded. To some extent, such power relationships reflect the status and standing of pupils in society. In England, children are not able to take on their democratic rights to vote until they are 18 years of age. However, the age of criminal responsibility in England is just 10 years of age, one of the lowest in the world. It is understood that children know the difference between right from wrong by age 10 and the law deems that the criminal justice system should deal with any errors of their judgement. In other countries, even though they may recognise children know right from wrong, they do not criminalise children's behaviour until they are older. Other age barriers of 16 for the age of consent and 18 for drinking and smoking give particular notions of how school-aged children are viewed. In England, all children must remain in school until 30 June in the academic year in which they become age 16. They must, then, remain in full time education, take an apprenticeship or take volunteer work alongside part-time study until they are 18. Thus, all their compulsory engagement with education occurs before the age at which they take on their democratic rights in society. In an educational context, which is defined by compulsion, to what extent does the pupil have any agency within the school system? How do we define their legitimate (peripheral) participation (Lave and Wenger, 1991) in a community to which they are compelled to be a part? Furthermore, in what ways do we help to equip them to be part of this community?

These are not easy questions to answer. The focus I offer here will do little to provide the answers the questions deserve. Yet, any attempt to establish, or re-establish, understandings of feedback must consider issues of power and position within the prevailing context. The educational encounter for pupils is not a democratic one. Pupils are clearly not equal with teachers. However, pupils have power over their interest, engagement and the internalisation of their learning. To forget this leads to little more than a delusion of what an agreed curriculum or an outstanding teacher can achieve.

Early philosophers thought hard about the importance of education in helping to ensure that democracy could function in society. Education was not so much concerned with external goals but about enabling people to develop the skills to reason and justify their thinking in and beyond school, and in relation to others, in order to take part in democratic processes (Dewey 1916/2011: chapter 7). This seems a far cry from the education system in place in the twenty-first century, and the very clear goals delineated in terms of subject knowledge to be acquired. Our education system is therefore not particularly created to develop the skills required for playing a part in a democratic society, even though citizenship education now has a recognised place. Neither does it seek to give democratic rights to pupils who are not yet considered able to take on such a position in society. It puts teachers in positions of power in the classroom over pupils, yet within the system as a whole teachers seem fairly powerless. Kreisberg (1992) recognises this paradox (9) and offers some helpful insight into changing the practice of power 'over' to power 'with' pupils. Here there is clear consideration of teachers working *with* pupils in order to develop different teaching and learning relationships, which potentially have a greater transformatory capacity for pupils.

In addition to Kreisberg's offering, additional consideration is afforded to conceptualising other collaborative relational processes through which teaching and learning can be explored. These enable a broader theoretical context for conceptualising feedback differently. Alongside a notion of power sharing there needs to be further formulation of how this might happen. If democratic principles seem to be beyond our grasp in the context of schooling, as well as the fact that relationships are with children, we need to underpin alternatives to democracy that might frame the nature of the relationship in which different feedback processes might be shaped.

## Deliberative communicative action as an approach for developing feedback

When further exploring notions of democracy there is a range of writing that considers *deliberative* democracy. Gutmann and Thompson (2004) give interesting insight into how such a notion offers a more specific and nuanced understanding of democracy. They highlight the importance of continual debate, not always coming to agreement, and the premise of mutual respect. They draw on Habermas' initial formulation of deliberative democracy. What is distinctive, and of particular interest here, is the use of the term 'deliberative'. Englund suggests that it puts the emphasis on 'mutual and carefully-balanced consideration of different alternatives' (Englund, 2006: 359). In recognising that education systems often provide what Dewey (1927) calls a 'weak public', Englund recognises that democratic ideals are difficult within such environments, particularly when children are involved. Thus, Englund suggests that a more useful concept is deliberative communication. This brings together Habermas' concept of communicative action (Habermas, 1984 and 1987) with the concept of deliberative democracy. A more in-depth discussion of the synthesis of Habermas' thinking together with Englund's suggestions for adaptation can be found in Dann (2016a).

Of significance within the argument constructed in this book is the way in which pupils can legitimately be supported and heard within the feedback process so that their views can genuinely be incorporated. It seems clear that the teacher/pupil relationship is not one of equality, and that democratic principles are not appropriate. Chapter 5 highlighted the importance of the relational encounter in which the teacher (a more knowledgeable other) helps to structure the Zone of Proximal Development in which learning would proceed in advance of development. Furthermore, chapter 6 recognised that ultimately, it is the individual that learns, and the consequences of education are for each individual. These may be collectively amassed for economic and social benefit (Chapter 4). Feedback, thus, has to work across all these elements.

Habermas' concept of communicative action (CA) is used as a conceptual backdrop which can be applied to how feedback might be constructed differently (Dann, 2016a). Together with the notion of being deliberative in terms of mutual intent, its relevance stems from its positioning across 'lifeworlds'. For Habermas, the emphasis he places on the notion of lifeworld (*Lebenswelf*) is central. Habermas, in his hermeneutic endeavours, recognises that each person's knowledge and understanding draws on his/her own beliefs that span three 'worlds'. These are the objective world, the social world (shared community) and the subjective world (individual's perception). Each has its own validity claims. Biesta's (2013: 4) consideration of what makes good education has implicit links to lifeworld through his priorities for the three key domains of education: qualification (acquisition of knowledge, skills and dispositions); socialisation (how we become part of existing traditions); and subjectification (the individual subject-ness of each person). The thinking here reflects the insights that have so far been teased out in the emerging argument in this book and evidenced by the conversations that pupils offer when they are given a voice to talk about themselves and their learning. In Habermas' terms, 'the structures of the lifeworld lay down the forms of intersubjectivity of possible understanding' (1987: 126). Recognition of the ways in which the three worlds will form part of an individual's sense making seems vital if we are to develop feedback in ways that are authentic to pupil experiences. Indeed, Biesta challenges the educational community to broaden its fixation with a knowledge-focused domain constructed around qualification. It is therefore important to bridge the theoretical and the practically possible. Feedback may be, or at least partly be, such a bridge.

The concept of communicative action (CA) builds on the notion of lifeworld and provides a route for enactment. Central for action is communication. The immediate link to feedback thus chimes strongly. For Habermas, the essence of CA is summarised as

> the interaction of at least two subjects capable of speech acts and action who establish interpersonal relations (whether verbal or by extra-verbal means). The actors seek to reach understanding about the action situation and their plans for action in order to coordinate actions by way of agreement.
>
> (Habermas, 1984: 86)

To some extent, this definition of CA can become part of a definition of feedback. It outlines the importance of reaching a shared understanding and agreeing next steps of action. In the context of feedback, this requires that the judgements related to learning that have already been achieved are jointly understood, and that intended next steps for new learning, with actions to enable this to be reached, are agreed. There are two distinctive components here: jointly understanding the 'action situation' and agreeing plans for future action. In an application to feedback, this offers a particular view of identifying learning (now) and future steps (next). Clearly, there is an emphasis on collaborative interpretation as well as agreement for future action. It points to key features of how the learning space is constructed.

Central to the arguments in this book is how the gap between learning 'now' and learning 'next' are constructed, and how feedback can be better understood and designed to help alter the gap. By drawing on Habermas' notion of CA, together with the notion of deliberation, we can build an additional layer to the conceptual framework already explored. Consideration of Vygotsky's Zone of Proximal Development (ZPD) in chapter 5 helped to shape how the space beyond current learning might be considered in relation to the processes of learning and development. Furthermore, within this space is a more knowledgeable 'other' and a relational communicative exchange that recognises knowledge, social and cultural differences.

Vygotsky offers little detail of how interactions within the ZPD are played out in classroom contexts. Yet, it is clear that the learning space requires a bi-directional relationship between teacher and learner and is founded on a complex set of interrelationships that are co-constructed. Habermas' thinking raises the importance of notions of both understanding and agreement, which seem essential within this emerging conceptualising of feedback. In keeping with Vygotsky's emphasis on participation and action, Habermas' notion of CA requires 'communicatively achieved agreement [which] has a rational basis; it cannot be imposed by either party or strategically through influencing the decisions of opponents' (Habermas, 1984: 287). This points to a different type of relationship within feedback.

## The hermeneutic problem within feedback

Inherent in seeking to determine new understandings of feedback for learning is the problem of who controls and constructs the learning gap which feedback seeks to shift. The deterministic framing of the learning gap outlined in chapter 4 seems to do little more than present a façade of conforming positions, behind which teachers and pupils game play (Keddie, 2016; Pratt, 2016). Feedback assumes that there is a particular understanding of both existing learning and future learning, as it attempts to guide the movement from one to the other. What becomes clear from discussions with children, particularly those who do not achieve at the expected level (chapter 7), is that the understanding and interpretation of feedback (and hence learning) between pupil and teacher are not always as they are assumed. Invitations by teachers for pupil engagement in feedback often become formulaic and tokenistic, receiving superficial acknowledgement by pupils who give very different interpretations and meanings than the teacher intends.

As the research discussed in chapter 7 reveals, tighter more focused feedback may not necessarily be helpful for all pupils. There is disagreement in the research literature on meanings and enactments of feedback (chapter 3), about the importance of differentiating feedback approaches and practices. What is important to note here is the way in which feedback is considered effective. If done statistically, using meta-evaluative tools yielding effect size, it does not reveal who it is most beneficial for, or in what contexts. What may be happening is that for those pupils who already demonstrate the 'capital' to be successful in school, feedback provides an additional tool that they can utilise. For those pupils who are less able to capitalise on school experiences, feedback may need to be more specially aligned. The key message is that taken-for-granted assumptions that pupils will interpret feedback in particular pre-determined ways are not advocated here.

Social constructivist priorities, which seek shared interpretations, understandings and agreement over next steps, are specifically orientated towards more than an exposition of the domain of knowledge within the world of the school. Recognition that different 'actors' will interpret contexts differently because of their unique 'lifeworlds', must be reflected in the way feedback is shaped and consideration of its possible impact. Thus, the processes of framing the learning gap that feedback seeks to influence, must be understood by all participants. Such understanding must therefore involve perception, rationalisation, communication and judgement. It also demands that all participants are able to relate to an 'other'.

As with the notion of democracy, which is rendered beyond the full grasp of children in western democratic societies, we must also consider the abilities that are necessarily contained in the notions of co-constructed reciprocal feedback that are being presented. Are children able to participate in processes requiring co-construction and negotiated agreement? There is a danger that new notions of feedback become another obstacle to learning. If new feedback strategies require specific funds of knowledge and skills for successful engagement, such processes might further disadvantage particular pupils.

To some extent socio-cultural theory is based on the assumption that all learning is built up by individual interpretation, which is based on social and cultural contexts, mediated by communication, increasingly characterised by speech. Of interest, therefore, is the extent to which children can make sense of these interpretations and articulate them. Inherent in these requirements are the development of speech, recognition of the perspectives of 'another' and levels of more abstract thinking. Any notion of feedback has implicit assumptions that the learner will take note of the information and judgements of another person on what they have achieved and what they need to do next. As discussed in chapter 3, the focus of feedback matters. Such considerations have not been sufficiently linked to pupils' developmental ages/stages. It is important to recognise that each participant in the feedback process needs to be able to take on board the view of another's, and decide what to do about this view in relation to his/her own view. This is not a passive event, but an active cognitive one in which participants can engage with increasing complexity. To some extent, involvement with feedback is necessarily developmentally sensitive. However, engagement with feedback can also be part of a learning experience that can enable greater skills and discernment in future encounters. Some further consideration of cognitive requirements for engagement in feedback is briefly outlined in the next section.

## Developmental foundations for co-constructed feedback

Within constructivist theory there is a body of research that considers children's conceptual development. Founded by Piaget's work and subsequently built on by key theorists such as Bruner and Vygotsky, there are clear notions of cognitive progression in children. Despite disagreement over exact mechanisms of development and even the precise order and timing of such developments, there is acceptance that certain conceptual developments tend to happen before others. There is no scope in this book to carefully argue for particular developmental sequences. However, of particular concern for feedback are the skills of considering another's perspective, being able to give reasoned argument, and for using higher, order thinking skills. There are also issues related to volition and moral conscience. Development issues thus relate to cognitive, social and moral aspects of a child's growth. This calls into question the extent to which children under the age of 7 can begin to engage in such processes. It also raises important issues about whether children between approximately ages 7 and 10 will benefit in the same way as those who are older, and have more advanced conceptual thinking. In seeking to consider how age may influence engagement in feedback it is not intended to offer a precise age-related approach for operationalisation. Rather, it is offered in the spirit of helping to recognise that engagement with feedback can be used as part of a learning process which will itself change with children's developmental shifts.

Habermas offers some consideration of the engagement of children even though his theoretical offerings are largely constructed as a meta-theory aimed at broader social, political and economic systems. Habermas (1990) devoted considerable attention to the importance of the development and application of moral consciousness as part of engagement with communicative action. To this end, he advocates that in order to negotiate meanings and form agreements on action there are both cognitive and moral strands required. Habermas draws on the work of both Kohlberg and Selman in order to tease out key development issues essential for participation in communicative action.

Kohlberg's theory (1981) is utilised to reveal the increasing skill in which children are able to argue, recognise competing perspectives and decide how best to translate discourse into action. In accordance with Piaget's theory, the importance of recognising the increasing importance of children being able to decentre and recognise the perspective of others alongside their own is highlighted. Although a progression of development is recognised, it is not linked to absolute ages. In addition to Kohlberg's theory, Habermas highlights the importance of understanding perspective taking in more detail. He draws on Selman's work (in Habermas, 1990: 141–144) who identifies perspective taking as developmental. From ages 5–9 children are able to differentiate concepts related to different people and they have subjective 'concepts of relations'. At the next level (2) from ages 7–12 children are able to look outside themselves and see themselves in the second person. They are also able to be self-reflective. Relations are seen as reciprocal. From ages 10–15 (level 3) individuals can look outside themselves and beyond themselves and see themselves in the third person. Relations then become based on mutuality (Habermas, 1990: 142–143). Thus, Habermas clearly tries to present a developmental theory which indicates that from the age of 5, children can recognise themselves as distinctive from others; their acquisition of language is complete by the age of 9. From the age of 7 they have increasing abilities to take on the perspectives of others and position themselves in more considered ways in relation to others.

There are some clear indicators here in terms of how feedback might be developed and enacted for different age ranges. Such differences might not necessarily be seen as discrete, but part of the development processes. Therefore, the way in which feedback is developed with pupils can increasingly become part of their learning and development process, affording new opportunities for thinking, reflecting and negotiating in ways that support them in becoming increasingly more confident and skilled. To this end feedback *for* learning can also be considered as feedback *as* learning (Dann, 2002 and 2014). As much as feedback is a process of establishing how to move from 'now' to 'next', there are significant knowledge-related issues that also need some clarification.

## How can you have a legitimate stake in something about which you do not know?

A key aspect of feedback is that it links the past, present and future (as discussed in chapter 2). Its greatest significance is its role in trying to direct and focus a particular future, which is specifically linked to judgements of existing demonstrations of learning. It is a tool for reshaping and refining an individual's academic identity. The elements of both assessment of what is already known and the knowledge about what should be learnt next, are typically thought to be the prerogative of a more knowledgeable 'other'. Such a view has characterised the dominant discourses influencing the relationship of teaching and learning in England and elsewhere. They are structured to shape and measure academic identity in particular ways. As indicated in the discussion in chapter 2, the positioning of both subject matter and participants in schools and classrooms is not straightforward, and is typically hierarchically structured. In outlining a social-cultural position, pupils are recognised as bringing significant and different 'capital' to their school experiences. Even within Vygotsky's ZPD, there is acknowledgement that there does need to be a more knowledgeable person, but this is not so that next steps in learning should be imposed, but to help align and co-construct learning.

Such notions of power sharing and co-construction are based on all participants having some notion of 'next' in terms of their learning. What was particularly interesting in the small-scale study outlined in the previous chapter (7) was that most of the children, who were all not making 'expected' progress, were unable to talk about next steps in learning in mathematics. In literacy, they had limited low-level ideas of what they needed to improve. This was despite the fact that they had target cards stuck into the back of their books. They had not internalised the targets and next steps that had been given to them. When given the opportunity to talk about their learning they struggled to frame it in the ways expected. Nevertheless, they were positive about school and were clearly trying to conform. What may need to be considered in more detail links to Lee's (2008) insights that schools need to make more effort in linking what children 'already know and value to what they do not yet know' (275). Crucial here is linking feedback to exiting schema (Nutbrown, 2011). This introduces the importance of finding out their perceptions, and their thinking, rather than imposing external priorities. But this alone may not suffice. Moll (2010: 456) asserts, 'when students witness the validation of their culture and language, hence of themselves, within the educational process, when they "see themselves" in their schooling, they combine their home or community identities with an academic identity'.

At one level, the communicative encounter upon which feedback is founded must allow pupils to share and reveal more than their 'academic identity'. If school knowledge is only seen as external to the individual learner, then feedback would be constructed only by those who can look in and make judgements about what is not yet known and direct next steps. However, as soon as learning becomes situated in real contexts, which are experienced and linked to prior learning in complex and often intangible ways, what is not known is understood differently. Instead of the learner being the person in deficit, disempowered to have any stake in judging or planning next steps, both teacher and learner can be seen as having different and partial knowledge. These different strands of knowledge may not be equal, but their validity in the process of co-constructing next steps in learning are. Within feedback there need to be strands of knowledge that relate to both the objective goal-orientated purposes of education as well as more propositional (or subjective) knowledge that relates more specifically to individuals. Such a view is foundational in Habermas' concept of communicative action.

As Moran and Murphy (2012) claim, such distinctive strands position Habermas' views as a 'philosophy of between'. That is between individuals' constructing lifeworld (the personal) and national systems. This is not an easy space to inhabit. In western capitalist society, economies and societies are structured to ensure that systems reproduce and gain greater dominance. To some extent, as can be seen in education, systems often colonise lifeworld and dominate it as their goals and priorities transcend individuals' ontology. Habermas, by promoting the role of reasoned argument and agreement, offers a way of rebalancing systems and 'lifeworlds'. This approach, to some extent, might be seen as a tool of resistance (Moran and Murphy, 2012: 176) which counters dominating performativity system-orientated discourses.

What has been argued so far, presents a challenge to notions of power and position of teachers over learners, and relocates school knowledge alongside more subjective knowledge, personally, socially and contextually situated. Such repositioning of ontology and epistemology must be accompanied by appropriate processes, which acknowledge both lifeworlds and system priorities. They must also recognise that each participant has legitimate and different perspectives to offer that are vital to the future that is constructed. Structuring feedback to help construct new learning in the future means that no one has complete control. The future is unknown and to some extent renders all participants differently powerless and powerful in what they might bring to engaging in processes through which the future becomes nearer and tangible. Critical and central to any such processes is the role of reciprocal communication. Seeking to reimagine feedback thus requires a different understanding of the form and function of communication within feedback. Essential as an initial premise is how language is developed, shared and utilised within the feedback process.

## Language and communication within feedback

At the core of education is the notion of communication (Dewey, 1916; Biesta, 2013). Its meaning, and consequently its application, are far from universally agreed.

If the way in which education is constructed with pupils is to be developed into the feedback process, which is designed to further enable learning progress, then further understanding communication within feedback requires deliberate attention.

In much of the literature on feedback, the dominant form of communication used is in written form. This even seems to be the case with younger pupils aged 5–7, many of whom struggle to read it. This is largely determined by the teacher for purposes that are more about accountability than learning. Sometimes it includes the opportunity for pupils to respond (see chapter 3). Such inclusion of the pupil in offering their perspective is often tokenistic and veiled beneath a conformist learning approach.

Thinking differently about communication in feedback is essential if a relational perspective, along the lines so far teased out in this book, is to be enacted. In drawing on Habermas' notion of communicative action there is a clear sense in which each person inhabits a unique lifeworld. Therefore, all participants bring with them to the educational experience different perspectives, knowledge and lived identities. Within feedback, therefore, each voice in the feedback encounter is different. Particularly, in this account, the language of communication does not contain a prescribed meaning independent of the context and interpretation of which it is a part. Seeking to understand shared meanings may be more easily conveyed through speech. This is particularly the case with pupils whose written language and reading is less developed. From Vygotsky's perspective, explored in chapter 5, speech was an essential component of the relational encounter in which learning occurred. But this is not straightforward in many ways. Many researchers and philosophers have sought to further clarify the relationship of speech and language to learning and identity. This was briefly explored from Vygotsky's thinking in chapter 5. A brief outline of some key thinking is offered next in order to give greater understanding and insight into how and why feedback might need to consider particular communicative processes.

## Dialogical and/or dialectical foundations of feedback

Establishing that meanings are co-constructed and shared is important within socio-cultural theory. Others, such as Bakhtin and his contemporaries, see Vygotsky's view of language and speech slightly differently. Volosinov (1973: 102), for example, highlighted the importance of speech, rather than written words, by stating 'meaning belongs to a word in its position in between speakers, that is, meaning is realized only in the process of active responsive understanding'. He likens the process to an electric spark between two terminals when joined. He points out that if you wish to see the light, the current (or verbal intercourse) must be switched on. More importantly, it must be switched on at both ends for a spark to be created. Wegerif (2008) draws attention to an important distinction in seeking to understand the role of spoken language within the educational communicative relationship. He teases out a distinction between dialogic and dialectic speech, which requires further exploration and understanding as feedback practices are considered.

Wegerif draws the distinction as 'dialogic presupposes that meaning arises only in the context of difference, whereas dialectic presupposes that differences are contradictions leading to a movement of overcoming' (2008: 359). In essence, there is a particular distinction, which is often blurred within educational contexts. The term dialogic is often used to embrace spoken communicative encounters in which pupils are actively engaged. Such endeavours have been zealously promoted (Alexander, 2008). Yet, this conceals more particular and important nuances. The distinction of dialogic and dialectic is mainly premised on the different contributions of Vygotsky and Bakhtin.

Vygotsky, as pointed out in chapter 5, seldom uses the word dialogic. His position is more firmly located within a dialectic approach. Speech is about moving away from merely 'being', or even being-for-oneself, but being-for-others. It is about considering all the apparent differences and overcoming these into an individual identity, which is mediated through monologic inner speech. As Bakhtin indicates, a dialectical approach is, after speaking, about removing all the individual voices and seeking one shared view, 'one abstract consciousness' (Bakhtin, 1986: 147). This contradicts with a dialogic approach, which recognises that for any meaning there must be inter-animation of more than one voice. Meaning is derived as much from the past, from which it is related, to the future for which it might be applied. It 'cannot be grounded on fixed or stable identities but is a product of difference' (Wegerif, 2008: 349). Thus, even new meanings and understandings remain linked to the voices of others in the dialogic process.

What becomes apparent in the context of developing feedback is determining what we are seeking from a relational communicative encounter of which feedback may be a part. Are we seeking the final 'outcome' to be an individual personal interpretation, located solely within the learner, and subsequently demonstrated by that learner for others to measure? This is perhaps the issue at stake. A dialectical approach offers a view where ultimately differences can be overcome so that the final internalisation of learning equips the pupil in a particular way.

Wertsch (1991: 85–86) argues that through a relational communicative encounter an individual can take on the views of others when they become part of his/her own intentions. For this he uses Bakhtin's notion of 'appropriating'. Thus, an individual appropriates different 'voices' so that ultimately they becomes his/her own. This draws parallels with Vygotsky's notion of what happens between people (interpsychological plane), which then becomes internalised through the intrapsychological plane. As discussed in chapter 5, the learning gap, in which feedback operates, is characterised initially and essentially as relational. However, this may be problematic if particular voices are appropriated just because they are louder and more dominant. Although this may be a short-term solution, particularly when feedback is used in outcome-orientated contexts, they may not be sustained in the long term.

Fundamentally, the ontological questions remain complex, and to some extent, unresolved. However, Wegerif points to Habermas, and his thinking around making reasoning explicit, as a useful consideration in moving forwards. Through such an endeavour, whether final decisions transcend differences or include differences, the communicative action can enable all participants to both think and act differently as a result of the relational communicative encounter. Ultimately, this is what feedback seeks to achieve. An important point advocated here is that feedback deliberatively embraces the differences that individuals bring to the educational encounter. Seeking to convey a particular view from one person's perspective will lead to particular voices being legitimatised differently. It should not mean some voices are silenced – quite the contrary.

What feedback therefore requires is for individuals to orchestrate the voices (perspectives) which influence them. This is quite a different emphasis from much of the research on feedback. This is a notion drawn from Holland et al. (1998). Theoretically and ontologically, it seems to have something to offer. However, logistically, there are still key issues that have not yet been resolved in how a more socio-cultural perspective on teaching, assessment and learning can legitimately feature in classrooms that are colonised by neoliberal practices. A significant argument here is that such practices already exist. Clearly, in the previous chapter pupils who were not achieving at the expected level were making sense of their own learning in their own ways. Although they were making references to targets and the subject matter of lessons, their understanding, however, was not what was expected, and demonstrations of their learning were below that required. It was through simple discussions with the pupils that these mismatches in understanding and expectation became visible. Thus refocusing communication in feedback to some extent requires a re-legitimisation of the perspectives that are already evident in the classroom. How this might be achieved is given some attention in the following section.

## Pragmatic considerations of feedback for learning

In the twenty-first-century educational context dominated by visible global performance and positioning (chapter 2), to what extent can an altogether different set of premises be incorporated into the context of teaching and learning? When solutions for education are often sought in terms of simple solutions that can easily respond to the question 'what works?', answers that are less contractible and more complex are more easily dismissed. The arguments built in this book are partly conceptual but point to practices that lead to more participatory practices for use in relational communicative feedback practices. To some extent the book offers a new strand for professionals engaged in teaching, assessment and learning to further contribute to their becoming more conscious of their own perspectives (voices) as they make complex decisions about their own participation in education alongside their pupils. In attempting to consider a more pragmatic approach for proceeding with feedback for learning, there is a word of caution. Insights into possible processes and practices are not intended to form simple solutions. Indeed, such prescription would completely negate what is being offered. The whole premise for the approaches to feedback being explored is centred around meaning and interpreta-tion, which is part of an individual's experience of education. Part of the approach being constructed is about re-humanising feedback, and to some extent education. It is about recognising the pupil is more than a potential statistic who will deliver at or above 'expected' levels. It is about understanding their lives, and their learning, and enabling their experience of education to develop their potential. The danger of eliciting a tight prescription of what feedback for learning will be, potentially, would undermine the premises upon which the book is built. An easy solution is more likely to be technicised and lose the humane approach, which is foundational.

Of significance, as some of the more conceptual thinking for this book is trans-lated into some key principles for practice, are the logistics of application into classroom contexts. Any principles for feedback, based on the notions of relational communicate encounters in this book, are likely to be time and resource intensive. They cannot be delivered for a whole class on a daily basis. As soon as a more reciprocal form of feedback is introduced on a whole class basis it soon gets reduced to a more formulaic practice that in many cases become meaningless. Mercer (1995: 82) indicated this in his seminal work on the Guided Construction of Knowledge. He highlighted that the educational discourse that emerges, because teachers have little time, is soon mismatched with the wider 'educated discourse' to which it aspires. The same caution is highlighted here. Teachers need to think purposefully and constructively about the ways in which they introduce, develop and sustain some of the particular strands of communicative feedback that are considered in this book. Particular thought must be given to the age of the pupils, the extent to which their learning gap needs to be adjusted for learning (in terms of school knowledge), the perceptions of interpretations of all participants, and each child's disposition to learning.

## Principles underpinning feedback for learning

The principles offered below are distilled from the preceding discussion. They are predicated on some key assumptions and specific positioning.

1.  Pupils' school learning is one part of their 'lifeworld'. Some pupils are more equipped than others to make clear distinctions between what is required for school learning and can appropriately gameplay within school, so that they can hear, understand and respond to the school's call for 'successful learning'. Others will find this more difficult. Therefore, feedback strategies will necessarily need to be adjusted for different pupil needs.
2.  Pupils, in the space that is created with others, 'experience' education. Edu-cation is situated, and it has both an ontology and epistemology. It is not merely about acquiring new knowledge. Feedback, even if it is intentionally offered in relation to school knowledge, must recognise that such knowledge is internalised as part of a wider experience of learning.

3.  Pupils have a legitimate position in the construction of their own learning. An agreed taught external curriculum has to be owned by each learner. Feedback should not be isolated from the person to whom it is directed.
4.  Feedback messages will be interpreted differently by participants in feedback encounters. Therefore, there needs to be a dialogic encounter in which different perspectives are shared, and interpretations and actions agreed.
5.  Learning is about taking a next step and subjecting all that you know and are into something unknown, but it also needs to be connected to what is known. Feedback provides a bridge between the known and unknown; it needs its footings in both.
6.  Recognising that there is a gap (or space) into which a next step is to be taken needs to be understood, shared and developed. It is a relational space, not a deficit.
7.  Feedback for learning links past, present and future. It needs to link each pupil's past, present and future, not just external considerations and constructions of the past, present and future.
8.  If there is no notion, a limited notion, or a distorted notion of 'next' by the person to whom feedback is primarily directed, progression will be restricted and feedback is of little use.
9.  Pupils need to have some idea of, and feeling for, a need to learn something new, which renders the feedback relevant and useful.

Each of these points raises significant considerations for how feedback is used and how participation might develop. There are no blueprints or simple formulas that can be created for widespread use. Fundamentally, the interactive framework for feedback will be unique in the moment of situated deliberative communicative action. However, in beginning to consider the principles above there are some practical considerations that can help to focus attention and begin to develop the relationships that give insights to both teachers and pupils about how learning might further progress. The suggestions below are primarily based on feedback ideas developed with pupils who are struggling to achieve. For these pupils, existing feedback often does not offer them much help. It is perhaps with these children that the time and resource can usefully be initially directed to new feedback approaches.

## Questions and strategies to help develop feedback for learning in classrooms

### Understanding pupils' learning gap

What do pupils say in response to a question such as the following: what do you think you need to learn next in (writing, mathematics, reading....)? Their response to this question reveals something of how they internalise their learning and the nature of the learning gap they construct for themselves between learning now and learning next, in different areas of learning. It is a pivotal question upon which feedback for learning needs to relate.

For children who struggle to articulate any notion, or have a limited notion of their own learning gap, it is suggested that further conversations continue in order to establish what sense they make of the task of learning. The following questions might prove useful in building up a conversation about learning which will enable a better understanding of a pupil's learning gap. It is suggested that the conversations are built up in a particular subject area, although this may not necessarily be the case. The following questions may help to frame the conversation.

What is it like to be you in your class?
What do you find easy in mathematics/English…?
If it is easy, do you still have to improve?
What do you find hard? And why?
When you find the learning is hard, what do you do?
What help is useful to you?
What help do you wish you could have?

## Focused approach for understanding possible pupil/teacher misalignment (for pupils who struggle to achieve)

A focused intensive approach may be used with a small number of pupils. Where pupils have struggled to identify next steps in learning, it is important to more fully understand how they are framing their learning gap. The steps outlined here are more time intensive, but should not be needed with more than a few children. They could be undertaken by a class teacher, student teacher, a classroom assistant or a support worker as an intensive activity for 10–15 minutes (at least once each week for a few weeks). The purpose is to tease out how pupils understand classroom expectations in relation to their own learning and priorities. The intention here is to find out the child's notion of what they need to learn next (if they have a sense of next). Also, to introduce next steps or targets that are teacher initiated (what the teacher wants them to learn next). The purpose of the dialogue is to try and better align both sets of targets or next steps.

Using 'post-it notes' in two different colours (approximately 3-inch square) works well for this process.

a  Ask the pupil to identify his/her views of their targets (next steps) in a specific curriculum area (maximum of four or five). Using only one colour of 'post-it note' write each target for him/her as the pupil articulates it on a separate note.
b  Ask the pupil to place these in the order of the priority that s/he gives to each. When the pupil has done this, write on the bottom right-hand corner the position of each target in the sequence s/he has chosen (1, 2, 3, 4 etc.).
c  Take the second coloured pack of 'post-it notes' and talk with the pupil about wanting to add some additional targets. These are aimed at shifting the

learning gap to be more aligned to school expectations. However, they need to be carefully chosen so that they can be seen to be in the pupil's grasp. No more than three should be added. Write each additional target on a 'post-it'. Talk with the pupil about what each one means, what it looks like in the context of school work. If this can be illustrated using an example from the pupil's own work, this may help.

d   Lay out all the 'post-its notes' of both colours (pupil's targets in one colour and the new adult-led targets in another colour). Ask the pupil to put these into one sequence in the order they chose to prioritise. Write the number of the order in the sequence in the bottom left-hand corner of each 'post-it' (1, 2, 3 etc.).

e   Discuss with the pupil why they have ordered them as they have. Note what they do with the adult-led targets and where they are placed in the sequence. This will help you understand the extent to which they see their understanding of learning aligned with the teacher's or merely conforming to what they think the teacher may want.

f   Stick the 'post-it' notes in the order the pupil has determined onto a piece of paper. Make this available to the pupil in the relevant subject area.

(Where there are significant differences in priorities, feedback dialogue requires a different next step.)

### If there is misalignment of teacher and pupil intentions for learning

When there is evidence that there is a misalignment of intentions for learning between teachers and pupil, feedback can become a communicative tool for sharing and negotiating next steps. To this end, feedback becomes dialogic. The communicative encounter within feedback needs to recognise difference and not pretend that the teacher's view can be superimposed over the pupil's. The use of dialogic principles can be useful here. Alexander (2008) gives some useful insights here as does the Educational Endowment Fund's (2016) Improving Talk for Teaching and Learning project, which develops these practices specifically with children who are more disadvantaged. Talk that allows pupils to narrate their views, explain their reasoning and their priorities also needs to be combined with children and teachers being given opportunities to question, evaluate, justify and argue in a safe shared space in which all views are valued. These suggestions within feedback mirror some of the properties promoted with dialogic teaching. Extending them into processes of feedback that evaluate and frame past, present and possible future learning needs to become part of this dialogic encounter within classrooms.

a   Using the 'post-it' notes which convey very different priorities between teacher and pupil there is a basis for continuing a purposeful dialogue which seeks to find common ground.

b    In the next two relevant lessons, help the pupil to highlight two or three targets from their 'post-it' notes chart (one from each colour (one pupil, one teacher) and one of their choice).

c    If possible, mark the work with the pupil asking him/her to identify where the targets have been attempted, or where they have been missed.

d    Ask the pupil to talk through what s/he has tried to do. Work through an example or develop what s/he has done within the context of the work being considered.

e    Use questioning that encourages the pupil to offer his/her own thinking and justification. (Techniques include expanding on what they say, taking a statement of something in their work and rephrasing it, asking a 'what if' question to the pupil about something in their work to see if s/he can reinterpret what they have done from another perspective (you may need to scaffold this process)).

f    Encourage the pupil to ask the teacher questions. The aim of this whole sequence of steps is to try to help pupils internalise what their next steps of learning might be, what they might look like, and why/how they should aspire to achieve them.

## Using feedback to connect past, present and future

The importance of pupils having a notion of a learning future is crucial in feedback for learning. Their ability to connect past, present and future in their own learning is often distorted in everyday schooling. For some pupils this is amply modelled throughout their school experiences, and they have a sense of themselves knowing new things, and developing in different ways. Other pupils struggle to project themselves in new ways that might be different from now. What becomes important here is that pupils are supported to see their learning in all three phases: past, present and future.

> *Connecting with past learning.* Very often, pupil exercise books and work are not kept beyond the academic year in which they are completed. This removes the best source of seeing learning in the past. Having some strategically chosen samples available that can be used by pupils as they are actively supported to engage with them is useful. This allows pupils (with support) to tease out how they have become different through learning. Helping pupils to articulate what they have learnt, using their previous work as an artefact, allows them to narrate themselves as learners who have progressed ... whose work now looks and is different. This is an important strand of feedback for learning. It specifically develops pupils' skills of metalearning, which involves thinking about their own learning and strategies for learning. Such processes are likely to help pupils to strategise better in their learning in the future (Mylona, 2016).
>
> New technologies through digital apps are also useful in helping pupils capture their own learning journey though photographs and brief comments about their work. These can be built up into electronic portfolios or learning journey

repositories. Currently, these seem more popular in Early Years settings in which learning is often visually recorded as it is more transitory unless photographed in the moment of action. These have much greater potential to serve learning than is currently utilised across all schooling phases. However, unless used productively as a source of how learning has progressed, and as a means for connecting past, present and future learning, then the investment in resources may be of little benefit.

*Connecting to present learning.* This is the area into which most time and energy on feedback is already invested. It relates to the other strategies already highlighted in this section. Little is done to help pupils distil what it is that they have learnt. To some extent, testing offers this. However, it often does so in quite a formulaic structured way that is easy to mark and which minimises the need to interpret what is said or written. One of the ways in which pupils can consider their new learning is by considering it in such a way that they can share it with others. This demands the use of higher-order thinking skills and is more suitable for children aged 10 or above. The process of extracting what you have learnt, how you have learnt it, and what that now means is something we seldom ask our pupils to consider. Engaging pupils in such endeavours not only offers pupils a way of consolidating their present learning but also provides an opportunity to help pupils who are younger gain a glimpse of their possible future learning (outlined below).

*Connecting to the future.* This is a tricky but crucial element of feedback for learning. The whole process is about moving learning forward to new futures for each pupil. It therefore renders feedback to be speculative and unstable. It also means that pupils, who are not experienced in school knowledge, are often regarded as ignorant of the future that others perceive them to need. How can you know about what you don't know? What is important in practice is that pupils have a notion of themselves as becoming different – as individuals who can imagine knowing different things. They need to have curiosity and a positive disposition for learning. Many of the pupils (struggling to succeed) in the small-scale study of 10-year-olds presented in chapter 7, revealed that they had little idea of themselves as future learners ... they did not know what they did not know! The tightly focused curriculum on offer to them, with clearly delineated success criteria, was not fitting into their thinking about who they are, what they were aiming for, or what learning was going to offer them. As a specific response to this, it is suggested that the notions of 'trailers for learning' is further developed.

*'Trailers for learning'* is a strategy that is specifically suggested here, which can help all pupils, but might be particularly useful for pupils who struggle to have a vision for learning new things. It draws from the media-driven practice of advertising, using trailers or advertisements. It offers just enough of something new and interesting to 'hook in' the viewer into something for which they had previously little or no interest. It is offered here as a means of introducing possibilities for future learning at a fairly general level. The focus might be to outline some new learning in the next year group rather than at a very tangible next step level for individual

pupils. However, more nuanced adaptions can be made to the idea as it is adapted in specific contexts. Two iterations are offered here.

a  Firstly, simple short films that showcase some of the learning that becomes available in each year group. Obviously there are national possibilities here. However, the preferred option is that these are developed in specific school contexts with individual schools or clusters of schools. A short 'film' or series of films are made for each year group. Using something like 'imovie app' or other simple film making applications is ideal. If it features the pupils within school and the work of known pupils in familiar contexts, this adds to the likelihood of pupils grasping this as a possible future for them. These are simple movie-style portrayals showcasing what pupils have learnt, lasting just a minute or two.

b  The second iteration is linked to the first, but is used as a means of one group of pupils consolidating their present learning by making a simple film of their learning for the class below. This approach has the added factor of enabling pupils to rethink and articulate what they have learnt in order to share it with younger pupils. It is appreciated that both these require investment in time. Yet, they highlight new possibilities for rethinking and enacting how feedback might develop in new ways that shifts learning forwards. This approach requires older pupils to develop their metacognitive skills and to present their thinking and learning to others who are less knowledgeable.

There is little research on such approaches in terms of the impact this has on the older pupils or those for whom learning futures is given greater visibility. It seems to be an area calling for some serious research action.

## Agreement and negotiating using reasoning

An important factor within assessment for learning is how feedback from teachers is interpreted by pupils as well as the extent to which it links with pupils' cognitive and emotional standing. Assuming that feedback will automatically convey the message(s) intended is not necessarily a helpful perspective. As chapter 7 revealed, for some pupils there is a clear disconnect between a pupil's priorities for learning and their teacher's. In some cases this may be that the pace at which the teacher progresses the curriculum is simply too far in advance of their cognitive progress. In other cases it may be that school knowledge is not a sufficient priority of particular pupils. Of course, there may be a combination of both of these. Teachers being more precise and more empathetic with their feedback is not likely to provide a simple solution. Rather, there needs to be a far greater effort to develop feedback as a relational practice, which engages pupils in shared deliberative communicate practice. This requires pupils being able to consider, reason and negotiate a way forward. It is a process that requires acknowledgement, rather than concealment of possible differences. This involves the development and use of their higher-order thinking and reasoning skills, associated with metacognitive and metalearning strategies. Furthermore, it requires communication in which different perspectives can be discussed. For this to happen, there must be 'power sharing' (Kreisberg, 1992) as well as a shared vocabularies. Some form of dialogic encounter that is genuine seems imperative, and allows and supports participants to think, reason and act.

Mercer (2000: 98) highlights the importance of 'exploratory talk' in classrooms. It seems to embrace the type of talk that could exemplify deliberative communicative action in the feedback process. Exploratory talk is a process in which 'partners engage critically but constructively with each other's ideas ... Agreement is sought as a basis for joint progress'. It is contrasted with 'disputational talk' in which other views are considered threatening to personal perspectives, and 'cumulative talk' in which different views are minimised. Seeking to develop both a context and vocabularies for exploratory talk seems to be an important step for making feedback more relevant and useful for some pupils.

It is recognised that one-to-one dialogic encounters would be impossible in a busy classroom with 30+ pupils and one teacher. However, for those pupils who are not in a position to align their thinking, and their actions with those required in a school context, it seems imperative. Furthermore, creating a space for all pupils to position themselves as active learners within the classroom community seems essential. Such a class community needs to facilitate an openness for learning, a shared space for being part of an environment where learning can be discussed, challenged, extended, and opened up beyond that which a formal curriculum so often constrains. This offers quite a different view of school knowledge than the one which is increasingly promoted in schools overshadowed by tests and examinations.

## Conclusion

This chapter has sought to establish a different conceptual basis for feedback. Primarily, it promotes feedback as a relational concept that demands reconsideration of power relations between participants. It recognises that feedback must be bi-directional with teachers and pupils learning from each other (intermental) and internalising new ideas and possibilities (intramental) (chapter 5). It requires action by both participants. Instead of feedback becoming a veil behind which both teachers and pupils assume their own meanings and hide or distort the realities of their own 'worlds' and priorities, it must become a reciprocal dialogic encounter. This demands a shared vocabulary, and a mutual respect in which negotiated deliberate communication about learning now and next is mediated and acted upon. It requires a pupil to understand 'what if' and 'what next', and an imagining of their own possible future. Feedback for learning must embrace knowledge (including that which is required for qualification and accountability), social co-construction and co-regulation, and personal priorities and vision. It is indeed complex, it is layered within social and policy frameworks, school accountability, teacher quality, teachers' professional practice, classroom lives and pupils' lived experiences of education. It cannot be rendered to simple notions of 'what works'.

# 9

# CONCLUSIONS

The concerns in this book have focused on ways in which future learning is planned, understood and enacted by participants in formative assessment. Its particular emphasis is on how feedback is used as a communicative tool in this process. This challenges and extends notions of feedback that dominate in the research literature. It specifically addresses issues of power and agency, through exploring who defines and controls the learning gap which feedback seeks to alter.

## Three conceptualisations of the learning gap

A particular emphasis in this book has been related to reconceptualising notions of a 'learning gap' so that there is wider scope for understanding its possibilities and limitations. The terminology of the learning gap, introduced by Ramaprasad (1983) (and subsequently by Sadler, 1989), was very much about establishing a gap, which needed to be changed or altered. Feedback was the mechanism that facilitated altering the gap. Framing the learning gap and the feedback messages used to alter it were very much seen to be in the control of teachers. Policy directives, increasingly drawn from global agendas, were seen to easily translate into the messages, and curriculum structures, which teachers created in classrooms.

This particular version of the learning gap I have characterised as the 'deterministic approach', and was the focus of chapter 4. It is clearly dominant within national policy and has evidently shaped teachers' classroom feedback practices. However, what becomes more evident within the book is the need to ask – who shapes and controls the learning gap, and for what reasons? The control within this deterministic approach is largely located outside the person whose behaviour and learning you wish to alter. This may be framed in an international or national context, when clear expectations and standards are explicit. Such 'zones of expectation' can frame the learning gap, and can seek to direct movement within the learning gap. However, it cannot control how a pupil chooses to alter his/her own learning gap in response to such expectations. A pupil must accept and respond to a vision for new learning which external expectation and standards frame.

As the literature on feedback (chapter 3) tends to be mainly dominated by research which seeks to establish 'what works' and what is most effective for increasing learning, particular concerns are raised that highly focused approaches may not adequately encapsulate the way in which all pupils make sense of feedback. Furthermore, it seems to marginalise or even miss other ways of understanding feedback, and may not be sufficiently helpful in terms of explaining how and why feedback is formed and enacted.

If feedback, initiated by teachers, were to have any impact in altering the learning gap for pupils, there needs to be some kind of shared understanding, and agreement of what this gap looks like by the different participants. This may easily be understood by some pupils, but, as revealed in chapter 7, this is not the case for all pupils. Chapter 7 illustrated how assumptions about the learning gap were understood very differently by teachers and pupils. For pupils who were struggling to succeed, it was very clear that they were not understanding or adopting the learning gaps and next steps for learning that teachers were constructing. They were downscaling or ignoring the feedback messages they were given to suit their own constructions of the learning gap.

Chapter 5 offers a different conceptualisation of the 'learning gap' as a relational approach. Such an approach identified the gap, which feedback seeks to alter, as possibly being seen differently by participants. The discussion was grounded in social constructivist theory, and particularly looked at Vygotsky's notion of the Zone of Proximal Development. The ZPD was already a concept that sought to make sense of a learning gap. Thus, more in-depth exploration of the ways in which the learning gap was understood through the concept of the ZPD offered an important focus for this chapter. By looking at Vygotsky's notion of the Zone of Proximal Development, possibilities were explored for how the relationship between teaching and learning could be differently constructed to recognise a more relational approach.

The space in which feedback occurs is framed as primarily social, it is between participants. However, the interaction of social (between) must also relate to internalisation (within). The interplay of these processes is not simple and linear, but part of a complex dynamic in which speech and language become the mediating tools. The argument developed in this book positions feedback in that mediating space which gives structure and purpose to the messages which shape learning. Both the teacher and the pupil are located as part of the feedback message. To draw on Holland et al. (1998), the teacher constructs the feedback by positioning his/her own professional judgement of where the pupil is (now) with the required (or preferred) trajectory for progress within the curriculum (next), and offers a narrative designed to enable the pupil to progress in his/her learning. The way in which the feedback is constructed and conveyed will of necessity reflect both a personal and professional teacher standpoint. It is both personal (it is a direct communication with the pupil) and professional (part of successful and expected teacher competence). It is also regulated by expectations (qualifications and standards) and it is also regulating (in seeking to regulate pupils' learning progress).

For the pupil, feedback is typically an external narrative related to actions expected at school. Pupils chose to align themselves to its messages and to adjust their actions accordingly. The great variation of pupil response to feedback in the literature may partly reflect the effectiveness of different types of feedback, but will also highlight the differences in pupil interpretations and intentions. Pupils cannot be assumed to be entirely focused on the feedback available to them, and they may choose to privilege it or marginalise it (or somewhere in between) for their own reasons.

Pupils' interpretation and response to feedback may be related to their intentions to develop their own cognitive capacities. Pupils will need to be able to link their next steps to their own schema, and to their own sense and purpose of being a learner. As chapter 6 argues, there must also be an individualistic dimension to the learning gap that allows for such an individualistic process. Furthermore, it seems likely that the extent to which pupils link new learning to current schema will not only relate to their exiting schema but how they make sense of their next step which feedback exposes. How it is constructed may be linked to a sense of curiosity that enables pupils to imagine themselves differently. Accompanying this envisioning will also be a feeling (a feeling of knowing – Loewenstein, 1994) that would need to be identified by the pupil as both safe and possible.

The way in which pupils are able to learn from others, who seek to build a purposive educational experience with them, would need to connect to their own constructions of who they are as learners and how they are building their own notions of the learner they want to be. If feedback is to be successful in helping pupils steer a particular pathway through a nationally prescribed curriculum against which certain standards should be met, the way in which the feedback messages, which can act as a pathway, are shared and communicated is unlikely to be available in a one-size-fits-all format. Pupils' lives are complex. Feedback is about a relational encounter to which all participants need to attune. It requires cognitive, social, emotional and action responses.

Also important within feedback is the significance of its narrative to its participants. As discussed in chapter 6, narrative has inherent notions of sequentiality (Bruner, 1990: 43). In order to relate to a narrative an individual must firstly understand it and secondly be able to relate it to his/her individual sequences or personal 'plot'. It must become part of an individual's personal learning story. Thus, feedback must be able to fit into an individual's personal understanding of themselves as a learner. This by no means excludes institutional priorities. Holland et al. (1998: 53) refer to a 'standard plot' that depicts agreed and established sequences which becomes part of convention, or in Bruner's terms, canonical. Within education there is certainly a notion of a standard plot which becomes an expected sequence of events with certain expected outcomes. As chapter 7 revealed, pupils may not share the same priorities as those promoted by an educational system (at a school and national level). They therefore may not focus on what is expected. Feedback can therefore become an instrument to help alignment. The learning gap therefore becomes less of a highly framed space, rigorously defined and specifically regulated, but a mediating space. Feedback functions in this space as a mediating tool in which the interpretations of all participants matter. It is multidirectional, and seeks to alter perceptions, understandings and curiosity for new understandings. As it is about the future (next) it must focus on 'what if' and what might be, and seek pathways that connect with existing schema, current and past experiences, as well as future imaginings. It involves an intricate intertwining of personal, cognitive and social threads. It is complex, unpredictable and multi-layered.

## Feedback for learning

The structure and form of feedback must certainly be targeted and purposeful. Knowledge required in the twenty-first century is part of the discourse in society. It is represented nationally, internationally and locally. There may certainly be some discussion over elements of knowledge, and its power and dominance in the curriculum. Indeed, the way in which the curriculum is structured, reproduced and recontextualised are matters of considerable concern and debate (Bernstein, 2000). So, too, are what is measured, and how priorities shift according to what is considered to be the best evidence for accountability. Such matters cannot be trivialised or marginalised in the discussion about feedback. They render the pupil fairly passive and powerless, and the teacher (with his/her pedagogic devices) as critical in order to bring about desired learning. The content of feedback must bear some relation to national expectations and agreed national content. It is each pupil's entitlement to experience education. Both feedback and the learning gap must therefore be aligned to, but not constrained by, overlying curriculum policy and priorities. However, no matter how focused the feedback, how directional the teaching and what is promoted in a national curriculum, a pupil must be able and willing to make the curriculum his/her own through internalising new knowledge.

This poses a challenging tension between knowledge and experience. The tension is not new: it formed a particular concern for Dewey (1938) who high-lighted that a pupil's experiences should not overshadow the content and goals of the curriculum. Dewey revealed his confidence in the 'potentialities of education when it is treated as intelligently directed development of the possibilities inherent in ordinary experience' (89). He highlighted the importance of a rigorously structured and ordered curriculum aligned with what individual pupils bring with them as they actively experience a continuity of their own school education. It is not a question of pupil-centred priorities replacing teachers' priorities. This just brings us back to the well-established polarised debates of progressivism versus traditionalism, or constructivism versus positivism. This is both unhelpful and only serves to illustrate how education is so often reduced to over-simplistic dichotomies which serve the short-term political instabilities which particularly dominate the education system in England.

The argument in this book has sought to explore feedback as a communicative tool within the school context of teaching and learning. It does so by exposing how the distortions created by a politically driven curriculum 'outcomes' approach, driven by international competiveness, steers the knowledge basis of education (including feedback) into particular directions. Feedback, if only focused on a predetermined trajectory of measured outcome expectations, may be unhelpful for pupils' learning. Other ways of understanding the learning gap that feedback seeks to alter, were also explored. The importance of recognising a socially situated space in which teaching and learning is a relational process, each participant having both a voice and a view, is a necessary component of feedback. This does not mean that each voice is equal or that any view is accepted. The relational processes of feedback must encourage the importance of a dialogic experience in which different views can be shared, understood and negotiated, and through which teaching (teacher) and learning (pupil) intentions are better aligned. It does not accept the view that knowledge is generated by the pupil. This is so often the conclusion when constructivist perspectives are considered (McPhail, 2016). Rather it promotes a view that pupils 'do not create knowledge but come to their own understanding of it' (McPhail, 2016: 308). There is a subtle but important difference here.

Feedback must acknowledge and function alongside the individual learner's cognitive and personal identities. It informs the teacher about how to recontextualise knowledge, link to existing schema, capture curiosity, lay out next steps. It requires complex interlinking of content, context and personal possibility. Feedback also engages the pupil in a dialogue about the possibilities for what happens next. Feedback must help the pupil make sense of the school curriculum so that it can be understood through the experience and context of education and become a part of the pupil's own developing identity. Such an identity is not confined to school; the feedback for school learning must also connect with the pupil's own narrative of himself and the person s/he wants and needs to become.

Feedback is not offered here as a simple solution, it is not reduced to a single set of techniques that allow us to answer the question – what works? It does not come down on the side of the teacher or learner, constructivism or positivism, progressivism or traditionalism. Feedback for learning is offered as a relational deliberative communicative process that requires participation and action by both pupil and teacher. It is focused on a learning gap and how it alters this gap. However, it is not simply about closing a gap. It is about understanding the learning gap, who controls it and why, and in which context and conditions it exists. One of the statements that promoted the writing of this book was from Torrance (2012) who problematised a linear notion of a learning gap. He claimed that

the issue is not so much to close this 'gap' in any straightforward sense, but to explore and exploit the gaps between teacher and student, and between students' present and developing understanding through pedagogic action, so that learners come to understand what are the issues at stake, and what learning means for them

*(Torrance, 2012: 333–334)*

It is hoped that this book offers something towards such a challenge, by offering reasoned consideration of feedback related to theory, policy and practice, enabling greater potential for the possibilities for learning.

# REFERENCES

Adcroft, A. (2011) The mythology of feedback, *Higher Education Research and Development*, 30(4), 405–419.

Alexander, R. (2008) *Towards dialogic teaching*, London: Dialogos.

Arendt, H. (1958) *The human condition*, Chicago, IL: University of Chicago Press.

Arnold, M. (1908) *Board of Education, reports on elementary schools 1852–1882*, with introduction by F.S. Marvin, London: HMSO.

Askew, S. and Lodge, C. (2000) Gifts, ping-pong and loops – linking feedback and learning. In Askew, A. (ed.) *Feedback for learning*, London: Routledge.

Assessment Reform Group (1999) *Assessment for learning: beyond the black box*, Cambridge: University of Cambridge School of Education.

Assessment Reform Group (2002) *10 Principles of AfL*, accessed online 10 September 2016, http://webarchive.nationalarchives.gov.uk/20101021152907/; http:/www.ttrb.ac.uk/View Article2.aspx?ContentId=15313

Au, W. (2011) Teaching under the new Taylorism: high stakes testing and the standardization of the 21st century curriculum, *Journal of Curriculum Studies*, 43(1), 25–45.

Bakhtin, M. (1986) *Speech genres and other late essays*, Austin, TX: University of Texas Press.

Barker, E.L. (2013) The chimera of validity, *Teachers College Record*, 115(9), 1–26.

Bennett, R.E. (2011) Formative assessment: a critical review, *Assessment in Education*, 18(1), 5–25.

Berger, P.L. and Luckmann, T. (1966) *The social construction of reality*, Middlesex: Penguin.

Berlyne, D.E. (1954) A theory of human curiosity, *British Journal of Psychology*, 45(3), 180–191.

Bernstein, B. (2000) *Pedagogic, symbolic control and identity: theory, research, critique* (revised edition), New York: Rowman and Littlefield.

Biesta, G.J.J. (2004) Education accountability, and the ethical demand: can the democratic potential of accountability be regained? *Educational Theory*, 54(3), 233–250.

Biesta, G.J.J. (2006) *Beyond learning*, Boulder, CO: Paradigm Publishers.

Biesta, G.J.J. (2007) Why 'what works' won't work: evidence based practice and the democratic deficit in educational research, *Educational Theory*, 57(1), 1–22.

Biesta, G.J.J. (2010) *Good education in an age of measurement*, Boulder, CO: Paradigm Publishers.

Biesta, G.J.J. (2013) *The beautiful risk of education*, Boulder, CO: Paradigm Publishers.

Black, P. (2015) Formative assessment – an optimistic but incomplete vision, *Assessment in Education: Principles, Policy and Practice*, 22(1), 161–177.

Black, P. and Wiliam, D. (1998a) Assessment and classroom learning, *Assessment in education: Principles, Policy and Practice*, 5(1), 7–74.

Black, P. and Wiliam, D. (1998b) Inside the black box: raising standards through classroom assessment, *Phi Delta Kappan*, 80(2), 139–148.

Black, P.J. and Wiliam, D. (1998c) *Inside the black box: raising standards through classroom assessment*, London: King's College London School of Education.

Black, P.J. and Wiliam, D. (2003) 'In praise of educational research': formative assessment, *British Educational Research Journal*, 29(5), 623–637.

Black, P. and Wiliam, D. (2009) Developing the theory of formative assessment, *Educational Assessment Evaluation and Accountability*, 21, 5–31.

Black, P., Mc Cormick, R., James, M. and Pedder, D. (2006) Learning how to learn and assessment for learning: a theoretical inquiry, *Research Papers in Education*, 2, 119–132.

Bloom, B.S. (1969) Some theoretical issues relating to educational evaluation. In Tyler, R.W. (ed.) *Educational evaluation: new roles, new means. The 63rd year book of the National Society for the Study of Education*, part 2 (vol. 69), Chicago, IL: University of Chicago Press, pp. 26–50.

Boud, D. and Molloy, E. (2013) Rethinking models of feedback for learning: the challenge of design, *Assessment and Evaluation in Higher Education*, 38(6), 698–712.

Bruner, J. (1990) *Acts of meaning*, Cambridge, MA: Harvard.

Bullard, T. (2016) I feel sad for my year 6 children, *Times Educational Supplement*, 13/5/20, 16, 8–9.

Butler, D.L. and Winne, P.H. (1995) Feedback and self-regulated learning: a theoretical synthesis, *Review of Educational Research*, 65(3), 245–281.

Carless, D., Salter, D., Yang, M. and Lam, J. (2011) Developing sustainable feedback practices, *Studies in Higher Education*, 36(5), 395–407.

Chaiklin, S. (2003) The Zone of Proximal Development in Vygotsky's analysis of learning and instruction. In Kozulin, A., Gindis, B., Ageyev, V. and Miller, S. (eds) *Vygotsky's educational theory in cultural context*, Cambridge: Cambridge University Press, pp. 39–64.

Clarke, S. (2000) Getting it right – distance marking as accessible and effective feedback in the primary classroom. In Askew, S. (ed.) *Feedback for learning*, London: Falmer/Routledge, pp. 32–42.

Cook, C. (2016) School system does not reward the best head teachers, *Newsnight* report, accessed on 20 October 2016, http://www.bbc.co.uk/news/education-37717211

Council of the Great City Schools (2015) Student testing in America's Great City Schools: an inventory and preliminary analysis, accessed online on 27 March 2016, http://www.cgcs.org/cms/lib/DC00001581/Centricity/Domain/87/Testing%20Report.pdf

Craft, A.R. and Chappell, K.A. (2016) Possibility thinking and social change in primary schools, *Education 3–13*, 44(4), 407–425.

Crooks, T.J., Kane, M.T. and Cohen, A.S. (1996) Threats to the valid use of assessments, *Assessment in Education: Principles, Policy and Practice*, 3(3), 265–286.

Crossley, M. (2014) Global league tables, big data and the international transfer of educational research modalities, *Comparative Education*, 50: 115–126.

Crossouard, B. (2009) A sociocultural reflection on formative assessment and collaborative challenges in states of Jersey, *Research Papers in Education*, 24, 77–93.

Dann, R. (2002) *Promoting assessment as learning: improving the learning process*, London: Routledge/Falmer.

Dann, R. (2013) Be curious: understanding 'curiosity' in contemporary curriculum policy and practice, *Education, 3–13*, 41(6), 557–561.

Dann, R. (2014) Assessment as learning: blurring the boundaries of assessment and learning for theory, policy and practice, *Assessment in Education: Principles, Policy and Practice*, 21(2), 149–166.

Dann, R. (2015) Developing the foundations for dialogic feedback in order to better understand the 'learning gap' from a pupil's perspective, *London Review of Education*, 13(3), 5–20.

Dann, R. (2016a) Developing understanding of pupil feedback using Habermas' notion of communicative action, *Assessment in Education: Principles, Policy and Practice*, 23(3), 396–414.

Dann, R. (2016b) Understanding and enhancing pupil's learning in schools in deprived communities, *Education 3–13*, 44(1), 19–31.

Day, H.I. (1982) Curiosity and the interested explorer, *National Society for Performance and Instruction*, 21, 19–21.

Department for Education (2010) *The importance of teaching*. White Paper: November 2010, London: HMSO.

Department for Education (2012a) *Teachers' standards*, London: DfE.

Department for Education (2012b) *Statutory Early Years Foundation Stage*, London: DfE.

Department for Education (2013) *The National Curriculum: framework document*, July 2013, London: DfE.

Department for Education (2015) *Commission on assessment without levels: final report*, London: HMSO.

Department for Education (2016) *Educational excellence everywhere*. White Paper, March, London: HMSO.

Department for Education and Science (1988) *Task group in assessment and testing: a report*, London: HMSO.

Dewey, J. (1910) *How we think*, Lexington, MA: Heath.

Dewey, J. (1916, 2011 edition) *Democracy and education*, Milton Keynes: Simon and Brown.

Dewey, J. (1927) *The public and its problems*, New York: Shallow Press.

Dewey, J. (1929) *Experience and nature*, London: George Allen and Unwin Ltd.

Dewey, J. (1938) *Experience and education* (1969 edition), London: Collier Books.

Dorling, D. (2015) Reported in Vaughan, R., UK is a world leader … in 'teaching to the test', *Times Educational Supplement*, 18 December 2015, 6–7.

Dweck, C.S. (1986) Motivational processes affecting learning, *American Psychologist*, 41, 1040–1048.

Dweck, C. (2012) *Mindset: how you can fulfil your potential*, London: Robinson.

Education Endowment Foundation, Teaching and Learning Toolkit, accessed online on 31 August 2016, https://educationendowmentfoundation.org.uk/evidence/teaching-learning-toolkit

Education Endowment Fund (2016) Improving talk for teaching and learninghttps://educationendowmentfoundation.org.uk/our-work/projects/improving-talk-for-teaching-and-learning#when

Englund, T. (2006) Deliberative communication: a pragmatist proposal, *Journal of Curriculum Studies*, 38(5), 503–520.

Foucault (2002/1972) *Archaeology of knowledge*. Translated by A.M. Sheridan Smith in 1972, London: Routledge.

Freire, P. (1998) *Pedagogy of freedom*, Lanham, MA: Heath.

Gamlem, S.M. and Smith, K. (2013) Student perceptions of classroom feedback, *Assessment in Education: Principles, Policy and Practice*, 20(2) 150–169.

Gee, J.P. (2000–2001) Identity as an analytic lens for research in education, *Review of Research in Education*, 25, 99–125.

Gibbs, N. (2015) How E.D. Hirsch came to shape UK government policy, In Simons, J. and Porter, N. (eds) *Knowledge and the curriculum. A collection of essays to accompany E.D. Hirsch's lecture at Policy Exchange*, London: Policy Exchange.

Gillen, J. (2000) Versions of Vygotsky, *British Journal of Educational Studies*, 48(2), 183–198.

Giroux, H.A. (1997) *Pedagogy and the politics of hope: theory, culture and schooling*, Colorado: Westview.

Goldacre, B. (2009) *Bad science*, London: Fourth Estate.

Goldacre, B. (2013) Building evidence into education, accessed online 1/07/2016, http://media.education.gov.uk/assets/files/pdf/b/ben%20goldacre%20paper.pdf

Goldstein, H. and Moss, G. (2014) Knowledge and numbers in education, *Comparative Education*, 50(3), 259–265.

Gutmann, A. and Thompson, D. (2004) *Why deliberative democracy?* Woodstock: Princeton University Press.

Habermas, J. (1984) *The theory of communicative action: reason and rationalization of society* (vol. 1), Cambridge, MA: Polity.

Habermas, J. (1987) *The theory of communicative action. Lifeworld and systems: the critique of functionalist reasoning* (vol. 2), Cambridge, MA: Polity.

Habermas, J. (1990) *Moral consciousness and communicative action*, Cambridge, MA: Polity.

Hanson, F.A. (1993) *Testing, testing: social consequences of the examined life*, California: University of California Press.

Hardy, I. (2015) Data, numbers and accountability: the complexity, nature and effects of data user in schools, *British Journal of Educational Studies*, 63(4), 467–486.

Hargreaves, E. (2007) The validity of collaborative assessment for learning, *Assessment in Education: Principles, Policy and Practice*, 14(2), 185–199.

Hargreaves, E. (2013) Inquiring into children's experiences of teacher feedback: reconceptualising assessment for learning, *Oxford Review of Education*, 39(2), 229–246.

Hart, S., Drummond, M.J., Dixon, A. and McIntyre, D. (2004) *Learning without limits*, Maidenhead: Open University Press.

Hattie, J. (2009) *Visible learning*, London: Routledge.

Hattie, J. and Timperley, H. (2007) The power of feedback, *Review of Education*, 17(1), 81–112.

Haviland, J. (1988) *Take care Mr Baker: powerful voices in the new curriculum debate*, London: Harper Collins.

Haynes, L., Owain, S., Goldacre, B. and Torgerson, D. (2012) *Test, learn, adapt: developing public policy with randomised controlled trials*. Cabinet Office Behavioural Insights Team, London, accessed on 27/11/2015, https://www.gov.uk/government/uploads/system/up loads/attachment_data/file/62529/TLA-1906126.pdf

Heitink, M.C., Van der Kleij, F.M., Veldkamp, B.P. and Schildkamp, K. (2016) A systematic review of prerequisites for implementing assessment for learning in classroom practice, *Educational Research Review*, 17, 50–62.

Hill, A., Mellon, L., Laker, B. and Goddard, J. (2016) The one type of leader who can turn round a failing school, *Harvard Business Review*, 20 October 2016, https://hbr.org/2016/10/the-one-type-of-leader-who-can-turn-around-a-failing-school

Hirsch, E.D. (2006) *The knowledge deficit*, New York: Houghton Mifflin and Company.

Holland, D., Lachicotte Jr, W., Skinner, D. and Cain, C. (1998) *Identity and agency in cultural worlds*, Cambridge, MA: Harvard University Press.

Holmes, E. (1911) *What is and what might be*, London: Constable. Full text can be accessed at http://www.educationengland.org.uk/

Hoska, D.M. (1993) Motivating learners through CBI feedback: developing a positive learner perspective. In Dempsey, V. and Sales, G.C. (eds) *Interactive instruction and feedback*, Englewood Cliffs, New Jersey: Educational Technology Publications, pp. 105–132.

Hursh, D. (2013) Raising the stakes: high-stakes testing and the attack on public education in New York, *Journal of Education Policy*, 28(5), 574–588.

Kashdan, T.B., Rose, P. and Fincham, F.D. (2004) Curiosity and exploration, *Journal of Personality Assessment*, 82(3), 291–305.

Keddie, A. (2016) Children of the market: performativity, neoliberal responsibilisation and the construction of student identities, *Oxford Review of Education*, 42(1), 108–122.

Klenowski, V. and Wyatt-Smith, C. (2014) *Assessment for education: standards, judgement and Moderation*, London: Sage.

Kluger, A.N., and DeNisi, A. (1996) The effects of feedback interventions on performance: a historical review, a meta-analysis, and a preliminary feedback intervention theory, *Psychological Bulletin*, 119(2), 254–284.

Kluger, A.N. and DeNisi, A. (1998) Feedback interventions: toward the understanding of a double-edged sword, *Current Directions in Psychological Science*, 7, 6–72.

Kohlberg, L. (1981) *The philosophy of moral development: moral stages and the idea of justice* (Essays on moral development, vol. 1), San Francisco: Harper and Row.

Koretz, D. (2008) *Measuring up: what educational testing really tells us*, Cambridge, MA: Harvard University Press.

Kreisberg, S. (1992) *Transforming power: domination, empowerment and education*, New York: State University New York.

Kulhavy, R.W. and Stock, W. (1989) Feedback in written instruction: the place of response certitude, *Educational Psychology Review*, (1), 279–308.

Latham, G.P. and Locke, E.A. (1991) Self-regulation through goal setting, *Organisational Behaviour and Human Decision Processes*, 50, 212–247.

Lave, J. and Wenger, E. (1991) *Situated learning: legitimate peripheral participation*, Cambridge: Cambridge University Press.

Lawton, D. and Chitty, C. (eds) (1988) *The National Curriculum*, London: Institute of Education.

Lee, C.D. (2008) The centrality of culture to the scientific study of learning and development: how an ecological framework in education research facilitates civic responsibility, *Educational Researcher*, 37(5), 267–279.

Lefstein, A. (2010) More helpful as problem than solution: some implications of situating dialogue in classrooms. In Littleton, K. and Howe, C. (eds) *Educational dialogues: understanding and promoting productive interaction*, London: Taylor and Francis, pp. 170–191.

Leganger-Krogstad, H. (2014) From dialogue to trialogue: a socio-cultural perspective in classroom interaction, *Journal for the Study of Religion*, 27, 104–128.

Leontiev, A.N. (1978) *Activity, consciousness, and personality*, Englewood Cliffs, NJ: Prentice-Hall.

Lingard, B. (2010) Policy borrowing, policy learning: testing times in Australian schooling, *Critical Studies in Education*, 51(2), 129–145.

Litman, J.A. (2005) Curiosity and the pleasures of learning: wanting and liking new information, *Cognition and Emotion*, 19(6), 793–814.

Littleton, K. and Mercer, N. (2013) *Interthinking: putting talk to work*, London: Routledge.

Loewenstein, G. (1994) The psychology of curiosity: a review and reinterpretation, *Psychology Bulletin*, 116(1), 75–98.

Lowndes, G.A.N. (1937) *The silent social revolution*, London: Oxford University Press.

Macdonald, I., Burke, C. and Stewart, K. (2006) *Systems leadership: creating positive organisations*, Farnham, Surrey, UK: Gower.

McPhail, G. (2016) The fault lines of recontextualisation: the limits of constructivism in education, *British Educational Research Journal*, 42(2), 294–313.

McMullan, D. (online) What is personalised medicine? Accessed at genomag.com on 1 June 2016.

Madaus, G. (1988) The influence of testing on the curriculum. In Tanner, L. (ed.) *Critical issues in education, 87th yearbook of NSSE Part 1*, Chicago, IL: University of Chicago Press.

Mercer, N. (1995) *The guided construction of knowledge*, Clevedon, England: Multilingual Matters Ltd.

Mercer, N. (2000) *Words and minds: how we use knowledge to think together*, London: Routledge.

Mercer, N. and Fisher, E. (1992) How do teachers help children to learn? An analysis of teacher's interventions in computer based activities, *Learning and Instruction*, 2, 339–355.

Messick, S. (1989) Validity. In Linn, R.L. (ed.) *Educational measurement*, Washington, DC: American Council on Education and National Council on Measurement in Education, pp. 13–103.

Meyer, H.-D. and Benavot, A. (2013) *PISA, power and policy*, Didcot: Symposium Books.

Moll, L.C. (2010) Mobilizing culture, language, and educational practices: fulfilling the promises of Mendez and Brown, *Educational Researcher*, 39(6), 451–460.

Moran, P. and Murphy, M. (2012) Habermas, pupil voice, rationalism, and their meeting with Lacan's Objet Petit A, *Studies in Philosophy and Education*, 31, 171–181.

Murphy, R. (1987) Assessing a national curriculum, *Journal of Educational Policy*, 2(4), 317–323.

Murtagh, L. (2014) The motivational paradox of feedback: teacher and student perceptions, *The Curriculum Journal*, 25(4), 516–541.

Mylona, P. (2016) *Metalearning: a contribution to theory and empirical investigation of year 4 pupils' reflections on their classroom learning*. Unpublished PhD thesis, University College London.

Naylor, F.D. (1981) A state or trait curiosity inventory, *Australian Psychologist*, 16, 172–183.

Newman, D., Griffin, P. and Cole, M. (1989) *The construction zone: working for cognitive change in school*, Cambridge: Cambridge University Press.

Newton, P.E. and Shaw, S. (2014) *Validity in educational and psychological assessment*, London: Sage.

Newton, P.E. and Shaw, S.D. (2016) Disagreement over the best way to use the word 'vaidity' and options for reaching consensus, *Assessment in Education: Principles, Policy and Practice*, 23(2), 178–197.

Nicol, D.J. and Macfarlane-Dick, D. (2006) Formative assessment and self-regulated learning: a model and seven principles of good feedback practice, *Studies in Higher Education*, 31, 199–218.

Nutbrown, C. (2011) *Threads of thinking*, London: Sage.

Obama, B. (2015a) Precision medicine initiative, State of the Union Address, 30 January 2015, accessed at Whitehouse.gov on 1 June 2016.

Obama, B. (2015b) An open letter to America's parents and teachers: let's make our testing smarter, 26 October 2015, The White House, Washington DC, accessed online on 27 March 2016, https://www.whitehouse.gov/blog/2015/10/26/open-letter-americas-parents- and-teachers-lets-make-our-testing-smarter

OECD information about PISA, accessed online on 27 March 2015, http://www.oecd.org/pisa/aboutpisa/pisafaq.htm

Office for Standards in Education (Ofsted) (2015) Key Stage 3: the wasted years? Accessed online on 20 October 2016, file:///F:/book%20back%20up%203oct16/book/Chapter%201/Key_Stage_3_the_wasted_years.pdf

Office for Standards in Education (2016) *Ofsted inspection myths*, accessed online on 22 September 2016, https://www.gov.uk/government/publications/school-inspection-handbook-from-september-2015/ofsted-inspections-mythbustin

Ozga, J. (2008) Governing knowledge: research steering and research quality, *European Educational Research Journal*, 7(3), 261–272.

Ozga, J. (2009) Governing education through data in England: from regulation to self-evaluation, *Journal of Educational Policy*, 24(2), 149–162.

Paavola, S. and Hakkarainen, K. (2005) The knowledge creation metaphor – an emergent epistemological approach to learning, *Science and Education*, 14, 535–537.

Palincsar, A.S. (1998) Keeping the metaphor of scaffolding fresh – a response to C. Addison Stone's 'The metaphor of scaffolding: Its utility for the field of learning disabilities', *Journal of Learning Disabilities*, 31, 370–373.

Peacock, A. (2016) *Assessment for learning without limits*, Maidenhead: Open University Press.

Perrenoud, P. (1998) From formative evaluation to a controlled regulation of learning processes. Towards a wider conceptual field, *Assessment in Education: Principles, Policy and Practice*, 5, 85–102.

Piaget, J. (1972) *The principles of genetic epistemology*. Translated by Wolfe Mays, London: Routledge and Kegan Paul.

Popham, J. (1987) The merits of measurement-driven instruction, *Phi Delta Kappa*, May, 679–682.

Pratt, N. (2016) Neoliberalism and the (internal) marketization of primary school assessment in England, *British Educational Research Journal*, 42(5), 890–905, doi:10.1002/berj.3233.

Pryor, J. and Crossouard, B. (2008) A socio-cultural theorisation of formative assessment, *Oxford Review of Education*, 34, 1–20.

Ramaprasad, A. (1983) On the definition of feedback, *Behavioural Sciences*, 28, 4–13.

Ravitch, D. (2010) *The death and life of the great American school system*, New York: Basic Books.

Richards, C. (2010) What has been, what is and what might be: the relevance of the critical writings of Edmond Holmes to contemporary primary education policy and practice, *Forum*, 52(3), 337–348.

Rose, T. (2016) *The end of average*. London: Penguin Random House.

Sadler, D.R. (1989) Formative assessment and the design of instructional systems, *Instructional Science*, 18, 119–144.

Scanlon, J. (2016) *Listening to boys write – an exploration of the complex relationship between 10 year old boys' writing practices and their evolving identities*. Unpublished PhD thesis. Manchester Metropolitan University.

Schmitt, F.F. and Lahroodi, R. (2008) The epistemic value of curiosity, *Educational Theory*, 58(2), 125–148.

Scrimsher, S. and Tudge, J.R.H. (2003) The teaching/learning relationship in the first years of school: some revolutionary implications of Vygotsky's theory, *Early Education and Development*, 14(3), 293–312.

Scriven, M. (1967) The methodology of evaluation. In Tyler, R.W., Gagnes, R.M. and Scriven, M. (eds) *Perspectives of Curriculum Evaluation*, Chicago, IL: Rand McNally, pp. 39–83.

Shain, F., Dann, R. and Watt, L. (2014 and 2016) *Raising pupil attainment in Key Stage One in Stoke-on-Trent Phase 1 and 2 reports*. Unpublished reports, Keele: Keele University and Stoke-on-Trent City Council.

Sharples, J., Webster, R. and Blatchford, P. (2015) *Making best use of teaching assistants, guidance report*, London: Education Endowment Fund.

Shute, J. (2016) Toby Little: the small boy who wrote to every country in the world, *Telegraph* online, 12 March, www.telegraph.co.uk/books/authors/toby-little-the-small-boy-who-wrote-to-every-country-in-the-worl/

Shute, V.J. (2008) Focus on formative feedback, *Review of Educational Research*, 78(1), 153–189.

Skinner, B.F. (1954) The science of learning and the art of teaching, *Harvard Educational Review*, 24, 86–97.

Speilberger, C.D. and Starr, L.M. (1994) Curiosity and exploratory behaviour. In O'Neill, H.F. and Drillings, M. (eds) *Motivation, theory and research*, New Jersey: Erlbaum, pp. 221–243.

Stobart, G. (2006) The validity of formative assessment. In Gardner, J. (ed.) *Assessment and learning*, London: Sage, pp. 133–146.

Tanner, D. (2013) Race to the top and leave the children behind, *Journal of Curriculum Studies*, 45(1), 4–15.

Telegraph (2016, May 3) Kids strike: councils warn parents could be fined for taking children out of school, reported by Javier Espinoza, accessed online 14/5/2016.

Thorndike, E.L. (1913) *Educational psychology: the psychology of learning vol. 2*, New York: Teachers College Press.

Times Educational Supplement (2016) Scrap Sats, say teachers – but pupils beg to differ, 13/5, pp. 6–7.

Torrance, H. (2012) Formative assessment at the crossroads: conformative, deformative and transformative assessment, *Oxford Review of Education*, 38(3), 323–342.

Torrance, H. and Pryor, J. (1998) *Investigating formative assessment: teaching, learning and assessment in the classroom*, Buckingham: Open University Press.

Tröhler, D. (2010) Harmonizing the educational globe. World polity, cultural features, and the challenges to educational research, *Studies in Philosophy and Education*, 29, 5–17.

Tunstall, P. and Gipps, C. (1996) Teacher feedback to young children in formative assessment: a typology, *British Educational Research Journal*, 22(4), 389–404.

US Department of Education (2015) Fact Sheet: Testing Action Plan, 24 October 2015, Washington DC, accessed online 27 March 2016, http://www.ed.gov/news/press-releases/fact-sheet-testing-action-plan

van de Veer, R. and Valsiner, J. (1991) *Understanding Vygotsky: a quest for synthesis*, Oxford: Blackwell.

van der Veer, R. and Valsiner, J. (1994) *The Vygotsky reader*, Oxford: Blackwell.

Volosinov, V.N. (1973) *Marxism and the philosophy of language*, translated by Ladislov Matejka and I.R. Titunik, New York: Seminar Press.

Vygotsky, L.S. (1934) The development of academic concepts in school age children. In van der Veer, R. and Valsiner, J., (eds) (1994) *The Vygotsky reader*, Oxford: Blackwell.

Vygotsky, L.S. (1962) *Thought and language*. Edited and translated by E. Hanfmann, and G. Vaker, Cambridge, MA: MIT Press. (Original work published 1934.)

Vygotsky, L.S. (1978) Mind in society: the development of higher psychological processes. In M. Cole, V. John Steiner, S. Scribner and E. Souberan (eds), Cambridge, MA: Harvard University Press. (Originally written in 1930.)

Vygotsky, L.S. (1981) The genesis of higher mental function. In Wertsch, J.V. (ed.) *The concept of activity in Soviet psychology*, Armonk, NY: M.E. Sharpe, pp. 144–188.

Vygotsky, L.S. (1987) *Thinking and speech* (N. Minick, trans.) In Reiber, R.W. and Carton, A.S. (eds) *The collected works of Vygotsky: vol. 1. Problems of general psychology*, New York: Plenum Press, pp. 39–285. (Original work published 1934.)

Vygotsky, L.S. (1998/1934) The problem of age (M. Hall, trans). In Reiber, R.W. (ed.) *The collected works of L.S Vygotsky, vol. 5 child psychology*, New York: Plenum Press, pp. 187–205. (Originally written between 1933–1934.)

Ward, H. (2016) I know our job is done when PISA is superfluous, *Times Educational Supplement*, 02/2/2016, 13–15.

Wegerif, R. (2008) Dialogic or dialectic? The significance of ontological assumptions in research on educational dialogue, *British Educational Research Journal*, 34(3), 347–361.

Wertsch, J.V. (1991) *Voices of the mind: A sociocultural approach to mediated action*, Hertfordshire: Harvester Wheatsheaf.

Wheater, R., Ager, R., Burge, B. and Sizmur, J. (2014) *Achievement of 15-year-olds in England: PISA 2012 National Report*, London: Department for Education.

White, J. (2014) *Who needs examinations? A story of climbing ladders and dodging snakes*, London: Institute of Education Press.

Wiliam, D. (2016) *Leadership for teacher learning*, Florida: Learning Sciences International.

Wilkins, A. (2012) The spectre of neoliberalism: pedagogy, gender and the construction of learning identities, *Critical Studies in Education*, 53, 197–210.

# INDEX